MW00558984

Standard Work
for the Shopfloor

SHOPFLOOR SERIES

Standard Work
for the Shopfloor

CREATED BY

The Productivity Press
Development Team

Productivity Press • New York

Most Productivity Press books are available at quantity discounts when purchased in bulk. For more information contact our Customer Service Department (800-394-6868). Address all other inquiries to:

Productivity Press
444 Park Avenue South, Suite 604
New York, NY 10016
United States of America
Telephone: 212-686-5900
Fax: 212-686-5411
E-mail: info@productivityinc.com

Cover concept and art direction by Stephen Scates
Cover illustration by Gary Ragaglia
Content development by Diane Asay, LeanWisdom
Page design and composition by William H. Brunson, Typography Services
Printed and bound by Malloy Lithographing, Inc. in the United States of America

Library of Congress Cataloging-in-Publication Data

Standard work for the shopfloor / created by the Productivity Press Development Team.
    p. cm. — (Shopfloor series)
  Includes bibliographical references.
    ISBN 1-56327-273-3 (pbk.)
    1. Production management.   2. Total quality management.
  I. Productivity Press Development Team. II. Series.
  TS155 .S7578   2002
  658.5—dc21

2002007449

06 05 04 03 02   5 4 3 2 1

Contents

Any company that is a leader in today's marketplace understands the importance of basic standards—rules for what is acceptable and what is not—in practices, processes, product quality, employee policies, customer relations, and so on. Standard work characterizes such an organization, in both its management and manufacturing activities. Moreover, the company practices standardization—it has processes for creating standards and standard work, for communicating them clearly, for maintaining and adhering to them, and for encouraging their continual examination and improvement.

In manufacturing operations, standard work is a key element in eliminating process waste and excess inventory and in achieving balanced and synchronous production. *Standard Work for the Shopfloor* has been written specifically to help your organization apply standards, standardization, and standard work to its manufacturing processes. However, throughout the text there is also guidance for how management can support these initiatives.

The information in *Standard Work for the Shopfloor* is presented in a highly organized and easy-to-assimilate format. There are numerous illustrations to reinforce the text. Margin assists call your attention to key points and other important features. And throughout the book you are asked to reflect on questions that will help you apply these concepts and techniques to your own workplace. Each chapter has a summary for quick review.

The "Getting Started" section suggests reading and learning strategies, explains the instructional format of the book, and gives you an overview of each chapter. Chapter 1 defines the key concepts and explores the elements of a continuous improvement culture. Chapter 2 looks at standardization by discussing the importance of clear communication and guiding you through the stages of creating, maintaining, and improving standards. Chapter 3 focuses on standard work and discusses its important elements and formulas. In four steps—using four key tools—it explains how to achieve standard work. It also gives guidelines for how to maintain your standard operations. Chapter 4 furnishes several helpful examples of the applications of standardization and standard work. Finally, a summary for implementing standard work is provided in Chapter 5, along with numerous resources for learning more about standardization and standard work.

To be competitive in today's marketplace, you absolutely cannot afford to let rules and work processes be haphazard or become customary by default. You must give conscious, quality attention to applying standards, standardization, and standard work to your manufacturing processes. *Standard Work for the Shopfloor* shows you how.

Acknowledgments

The development of *Standard Work for the Shopfloor* has been a team effort. Judith Allen, now Vice President of Product Development for Productivity Inc., initially spearheaded the expansion of the Shopfloor Series, including this title. As Publisher, I will continue to bring important and needed topics to this series. Special thanks are due to Diane Asay of LeanWisdom for shaping and writing the content. Stephen Scates of Graphiquorum Design Services created the cover design, with cover illustration provided by Gary Ragaglia of Metro Design. Mary Junewick coordinated the many project tasks and did the copyediting. Lorraine Millard created the numerous illustrations. Guy Boster created the cartoons. Typesetting and layout was done by Bill Brunson of Typography Services. Mike Ryder was our proofreader. And Bob Cooper managed the print process. Finally, thanks to Karen Gaines and Michael O'Neill of the marketing department for their promotional efforts.

We are very pleased to bring you this addition to our Shopfloor Series and wish you continued and increasing success on your lean journey.

Maura May
Publisher

The Purpose of This Book

Key Point

Standard Work for the Shopfloor was written to give you the information you need to participate in implementing standardization and standard work in your workplace. You are a valued member of your company's team; your knowledge, support, and participation are essential to the success of any major effort in your organization.

You may be reading this book because your team leader or manager asked you to do so. Or you may be reading it because you think it will provide information that will help you in your work. By the time you finish Chapter 1, you will have a better idea of how the information in this book can help you and your company eliminate waste and serve your customers more effectively.

What This Book Is Based On

BACKGROUND
INFO

This book is about an approach to implementing standardization and standard work methods designed to eliminate waste from production processes. The methods and goals discussed here are closely related to the lean manufacturing system developed at Toyota Motor Company. Since 1979, Productivity, Inc. has brought information about these approaches to the United States through publications, events, training, and consulting. Today, top companies around the world are applying lean manufacturing principles to sustain their competitive edge.

Standard Work for the Shopfloor draws on a wide variety of Productivity's resources. Its aim is to present the main concepts and steps of implementing standards in a simple, illustrated format that is easy to read and understand.

Two Ways to Use This Book

There are at least two ways to use this book:

1. As the reading material for a learning group or study group process within your company.

2. For learning on your own.

Your company may decide to design its own learning group process based on *Standard Work for the Shopfloor*. Or, you may read this book for individual learning without formal group discussion. Either way, you will learn valuable concepts and techniques to apply to your daily work.

How to Get the Most Out of Your Reading

Becoming Familiar with This Book as a Whole

There are a few steps you can follow to make it easier to absorb the information in this book. Take as much time as you need to become familiar with the material. First, get a "big picture" view of the book by doing the following:

How-to Steps

1. Scan the "Table of Contents" to see how *Standard Work for the Shopfloor* is arranged.

2. Read the rest of this introductory section for an overview of the book's contents.

3. Flip through the book to get a feel for its style, flow, and design. Notice how the chapters are structured and glance at the illustrations.

Becoming Familiar with Each Chapter

After you have a sense of the overall structure of *Standard Work for the Shopfloor*, prepare yourself to study one chapter at a time. For each chapter, we suggest you follow these steps to get the most out of your reading:

How-to Steps

1. Read the "Chapter Overview" on the first page to see what the chapter will cover.

2. Flip through the chapter, looking at the way it is laid out. Notice the bold headings and the key points flagged in the margins.

3. Now read the chapter. How long this takes depends on what you already know about the content and what you are trying to get out of your reading. Enhance your reading by doing the following:

- Use the margin assists to help you follow the flow of information.

- If the book is your own, use a highlighter to mark key information and answers to your questions about the material. If the book is not your own, take notes on a separate piece of paper.

- Answer the "Take Five" questions in the text. These will help you absorb the information by reflecting on how you might apply it to your own workplace.

4. Read the "Summary" at the end of the chapter to reinforce what you have learned. If you read something in the summary that you don't remember, find that section in the chapter and review it.

5. Finally, read the "Reflections" questions at the end of the chapter. Think about these questions and write down your answers.

How a Reading Strategy Works

When reading a book, many people think they should start with the first word and read straight through until the end. This is not usually the best way to learn from a book. The steps that were just presented for how to read this book are a strategy for making your reading easier, more fun, and more effective.

Key Point

Reading strategy is based on two simple points about the way people learn. The first point is this: *It's difficult for your brain to absorb new information if it does not have a structure to place it in.* As an analogy, imagine trying to build a house without first putting up a framework.

Like building a frame for a house, you can give your brain a framework for the new information in the book by getting an overview of the contents and then flipping through the materials. Within each chapter, you repeat this process on a smaller scale by reading the overview, key points, and headings before reading the text.

Key Point

The second point about learning is this: *It is a lot easier to learn if you take in the information one layer at a time, instead of trying to absorb it all at once.* It's like finishing the walls of a house: First you lay down a coat of primer. When it's dry, you apply a coat of paint, and later a final finish coat.

Using the Margin Assists

As you've noticed by now, this book uses small images called *margin assists* to help you follow the information in each chapter. There are six types of margin assists:

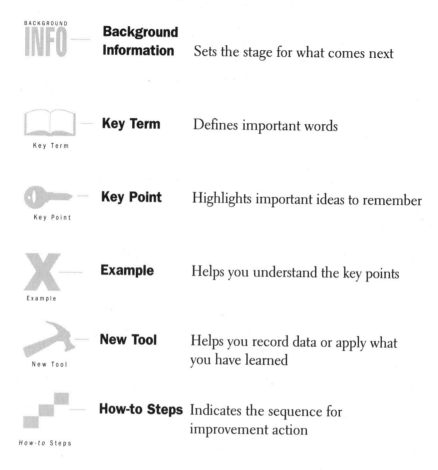

Background Information	Sets the stage for what comes next
Key Term	Defines important words
Key Point	Highlights important ideas to remember
Example	Helps you understand the key points
New Tool	Helps you record data or apply what you have learned
How-to Steps	Indicates the sequence for improvement action

An Overview of the Contents

Getting Started (pages xi–xv)

This is the section you have been reading. It has already explained the purpose of *Standard Work for the Shopfloor* and how it was written. Then it shared tips for getting the most out of your reading. Now, it will present a brief description of each chapter.

Chapter 1: Standards and Beyond (pages 1–12)

Chapter 1 defines the key terms: standard, standardization, and standard work. It explores the elements of a continuous improvement culture and describes standard work as the culmination of lean production implementation.

Chapter 2: Standardization (pages 13–33)

Chapter 2 describes standardization in more detail, discusses the importance of clear presentation of information about standards and how to adhere to them, and walks through the critical steps of creating, maintaining, and improving standards.

Chapter 3: Standard Work (pages 35–57)

Chapter 3 defines standard work and describes the key formulas for calculating takt time, end-of-line rate, work sequence, standard work-in-process, and cell staffing through line balancing. It then details a four-step process of establishing standard operations, and describes how to use the various tables and work sheets to create standard operations.

Chapter 4: Applications of Standardization and Standard Work (pages 59–76)

Chapter 4 provides several examples of the applications of standardization and standard work. Applications to employee training, design, making improvements, production management, and decision-making are discussed. Production management for small lots and level loads is also discussed.

Chapter 5: Reflections and Conclusions (pages 77–84)

Chapter 5 presents reflections on and conclusions to this book. It includes a summary of the steps for standard work implementation. It also describes opportunities for further learning about techniques related to standardization and standard work.

Chapter 1

Standards and Beyond

What Is a Standard?

Key Term

A *standard* is *a rule or example that provides clear expectations.* Continuous improvement methods depend on identifying, setting, and improving standards. Without an initial standard, how can you measure the effectiveness of the improvements you make to achieve that standard? How can you improve the standard? How can you set additional goals and know if you have achieved them? Standards form the *baseline* for all improvement activities, and they define the *breakthrough goals* you strive to achieve as your continuous improvement activities gain momentum.

In manufacturing, standards are applied to two aspects of production:

1. Product specifications and quality, to eliminate defects in products.

2. Production process analysis and improvement, to eliminate all process waste, which also includes defective products.

Characteristics of Standards

Key Point

Standards must be specific and scientific—meaning that they are based on facts and analysis, not on custom, guessing, or memory.

Key Point

Standards must be adhered to; they are useless if no one follows them. For a standard to be a standard, it will be *consistently followed and respected.*

Example

An example of a standard in traffic regulation is a red light at an intersection. What makes this a standard is that people actually stop when the light turns red. Accidents occur when the standard is not followed.

Example

Another example is a four-way stop sign. When two cars come to an intersection at once, the person on the right has the right-of-way. If the two drivers don't know this rule, then they may sit there for a long time wondering what to do, or they both may go at once and cause an accident.

Key Point

This describes a third characteristic of standards—*standards must be documented and communicated so that people will know what they are and can follow them.*

Sources and Types of Standards

There are three sources of standards:

1. Those based on authority, custom, or consensus that continually evolve over time.

2. Those based on scientific data or experience that change, but more slowly.

3. Those based on technical specifications that tend to remain constant.

Figure 1-1 shows many types of quality standards that exist in the flow of work. This book focuses primarily on *in-house* standards.

TAKE FIVE

Take five minutes to think about these questions and to write down your answers:

1. What are some standards based on *custom* in your workplace?
2. Which ones do you think need improvement?

What Is Standardization?

Key Term

Standardization is *the practice of setting, communicating, following, and improving standards.* Manufacturing processes depend on standardization. It promotes consistency through uniform criteria and practices. In 5S, the fourth S is "standardize"—make rules for maintaining the improvements achieved in the first three Ss. First you improve your process, then you standardize it: you *define the process* so that everyone knows what it is and can follow it.

In continuous improvement you measure the effects of your improvements in relation to the results of the initial standard. If you get better results with the improved process, then the standard can be changed. If the results are not better, the standard should remain. In this way, standards require you to prove, with facts, that the changes you make actually improve the process. Without the standard to measure against, there would be no process you could depend on, and no way to know how to improve it or whether or not you had improved it. *This process of continually improving the standards is the path to reliable methods—the*

Key Point

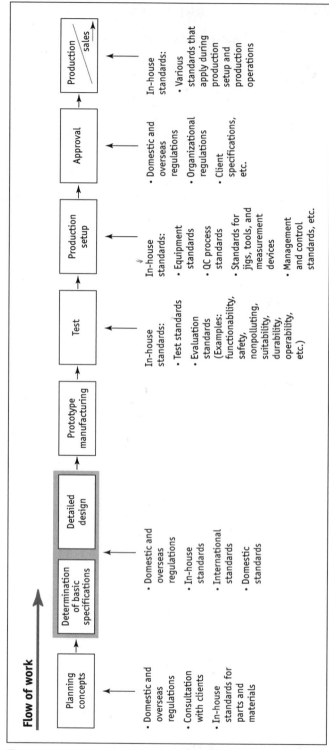

Figure 1-1. Flow of Work and Types of Quality Standards

effective and efficient sequence of operations that is a key component of standard work.

Key Point

Everyone must practice the standards consistently before standardization truly exists. Consequently, standardization depends on user-friendly language, pictures, or symbols to communicate the standard. It must be easy to see and understand what the standard is so that everyone can learn to practice it. *When 100 percent adherence to reliable methods occurs, you have standardization.*

In Figure 1-2 you can see that there are a number of levels to achieving standardization throughout the organization for its full benefits to be felt. Most organizations have achieved levels 1 and 2—the bottom two rungs of the ladder of standardization. When lean production is implemented and standardization of these reliable methods is achieved, standards are built into the objects of production themselves as shown in the third, fourth, and fifth rungs of the ladder. Standardized management methods are the final rung of the standardization ladder.

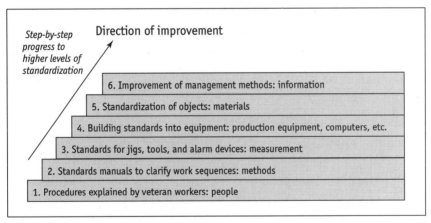

Figure 1-2. The Implementation Ladder of Standardization

TAKE FIVE

Take five minutes to think about these questions and to write down your answers:

1. Does everyone follow the standards set for your production line? Do you?
2. Can you identify one standard that needs greater adherence to be effective?

Aspects of standardization are described in greater detail in Chapter 2.

What Is Standard Work?

Key Term

Key Point

Standard work is an agreed-upon set of work procedures that establish the best and most reliable methods and sequences for each process and each worker. It is also a method that helps determine those methods and sequences. Standard work aims to maximize performance while minimizing waste in *each person's* operation and workload. Standard work is not a rigid "work standard" that never changes; rather, *standard work is the fluctuating level of optimum work to be done by people and machines each day to meet customer demand.* It is determined precisely, through a series of calculations, so that takt time can be adhered to by each operator and every line or cell. Optimum work in process and inventory levels, cycle time, and cell layouts are all considered in the standard work method.

Lean Manufacturing Methods = Standard Processes and Reliable Methods

Key Point

Standard work is a tool used in cellular manufacturing and pull production to best utilize people and machines while keeping the rhythm of production tied to the flow of customer orders.

We have discussed standards and standardization and reliable methods as the basis of continuous improvement. The set of methods that comprise lean manufacturing (5S, quick changeover, mistake-proofing, etc.) are themselves considered to be the reliable methods of production. You may find ways to improve or adjust these methods for your own workplace, but these already have been proven to be reliable. This means that wherever they are applied, in whatever culture, and for whatever product being made, these methods work—they are methods designed to create products at the lowest cost, in the shortest time, and with the highest quality. They ensure safety and support human autonomy and creativity. They deliver to the customer what he wants, when he wants it, and in the required quantity. Standard work is driven by improvement; it is not a rigid, unchanging rule but *a flexible response to current conditions in the workplace and in the market.*

Standard Work Is the Culmination of Lean Production

Standard work follows the implementation of cellular manufacturing and the initiation of pull production. Once these lean production methods are in place in your factory, standard work can be used to maintain them. Standard work, in other words, is *the final stage of implementing lean production.*

Prerequisites of Standard Work

Implementation of all the other tools in the lean production method is consequently the prerequisite to implementing standard work. They are:

- 5S and visual control
- Quick changeover
- Mistake-proofing
- Total productive maintenance (TPM)
- Jidoka—human automation
- Cellular manufacturing
- Pull production with kanban
- Load leveling and line balancing
- Multi-process operations and multi-task operators

Standard Work Drives Further Improvement

Key Point

Standard work functions as a diagnostic tool, exposing problems and inspiring continual improvement. It supports process standardization and further elimination of waste throughout the production process. With standard work in place, everyone becomes a detective, continually finding and removing waste from the workplace.

TAKE FIVE

Take five minutes to think about these questions and to write down your answers:

1. What is a reliable method? Why is lean production a set of reliable methods?
2. What are some characteristics of standard work?

7

Figure 1-3. Standard Work Makes Everyone a Detective

Chapters 3 and 4 describe the standard work calculations and documentation in detail.

A Culture of Continuous Improvement

In this chapter we have mentioned numerous characteristics of standardization and standard work. These characteristics can be summarized as being:

1. An agreed-upon best way to perform each operation and process: the documented standards and standard work procedures.

2. The discipline to adhere to the standards: standardization.

3. A mechanism for improving the documented reliable method: formal idea generation and continuous improvement methods.

A culture of continuous improvement should already be in place if you are implementing lean production in your plant or work area. This means that there are formal methods practiced by everyone for improving operations: weekly team activities, documented process analysis, and mechanisms for gathering data, reporting findings, and gaining approval for making changes in the current methods. Figure 1-4 shows that there are many control points for improving standards throughout the production process.

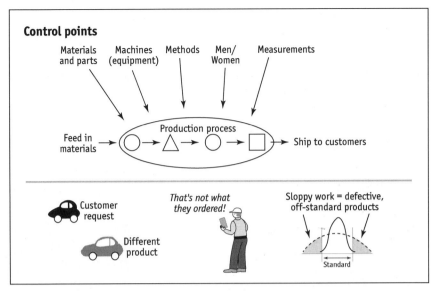

Figure 1-4. Elements for Building Quality into Products

Operators are continually thinking of ways to improve the way they do their work. The culture must support this creative problem solving if standardization is to be achieved and the flexibility of standard work is to be possible. What can you do to support continuous improvement within the context of standardized and standard work environments?

1. Support teamwork and ownership of the process by every operator.

2. Reward operators who make improvements.

3. Allow (don't punish) mistakes and encourage experimentation.

4. Create a system for capturing and implementing employee suggestions.

5. Provide collaboration with specialists to support the team improvement activities of cells.

6. Offer training to every operator on improvement methods.

It is important to recognize a critical and perhaps unexpected characteristic of creating standards, standardization, and standard work: they are not only the *result* of initial improvement activities, they also *drive continual improvement*. However, the improvements made must be based on data gathered from the baseline of the standard that has been described, agreed-upon, and adhered to by all. *Only when you have standardization can you systematically improve your operations without creating chaos, and thereby gain adherence throughout the system when a better way is discovered.* Standard work itself is intended to provide a flexible and responsive workplace, where operators can move to the operations most needed to meet customer demand. Without standardization—adherence to the set standards—this orderly flexibility and responsiveness will be impossible to achieve.

Key Point

TAKE FIVE

Take five minutes to think about these questions and to write down your answers:

1. What is needed for a culture of continuous improvement to exist?
2. Which of these is in place in your workplace?

The Benefits of Standardization and Standard Work

For the Company

Standardization and standard work benefit your company by enabling:

- Reduced variability, reduced waste, and reduced costs
- Improved quality and shorter, more predictable lead times
- The achievement of ISO certification

For the Operator

Standardization and standard work benefit you by making it:

- Easier for you to learn new operations
- Easier for you to shift to different operations within a cell or to shift to operations in other cells, lines, or work areas
- Easier for you to see problems and contribute improvement ideas

In Conclusion

SUMMARY

A *standard* is *a rule or example that provides clear expectations.* Continuous improvement methods depend on identifying, setting, and improving standards. Standards form the *baseline* for all improvement activities, and they define the *breakthrough goals* you strive to achieve as your continuous improvement activities gain momentum. *Standards must be specific and scientific*—meaning that they are based on facts and analysis, not on custom, guessing, or memory. *Standards must be adhered to*; they are useless if no one follows them. For a standard to be a standard, it will be *consistently followed and respected.* Also, *standards must be documented and communicated so that people will know what they are and can follow them.*

Standardization is *the practice of setting, communicating, following, and improving standards.* Manufacturing processes depend on standardization. It promotes consistency through uniform criteria and practices. In 5S, the fourth S is "standardize"—make the rules for maintaining the improvements achieved in the first three Ss. First you improve your process, then you standardize it: you *define the process* so that everyone knows what it is and can follow it. *Everyone must practice the standards consistently before standardization truly exists.*

Standard work is *an agreed-upon set of work procedures that establish the best and most reliable methods and sequences for each process and each worker.* It is also a method that helps determine those methods and sequences. Standard work aims to maximize performance while minimizing waste in *each person's* operation and workload. Standard work is not a rigid "work standard" that never changes; rather, *standard work is the fluctuating level of optimum work to be done by people and machines each day to meet customer demand.* It is determined precisely, through a series of calculations, so that takt time can be adhered to by each operator and every line or cell. Optimum work in process and inventory levels, cycle time, and cell layouts are all considered in the standard work method. *Standard work is a tool used in cellular manufacturing and pull production to best utilize people and machines while keeping the rhythm of production tied to the flow of customer orders. It is a flexible response to current conditions in the workplace and in the market.*

It is important to recognize a critical and perhaps unexpected characteristic of creating standards, standardization, and standard work: they are not only the *result* of initial improvement activities; they also *drive continual improvement. Only when you have standardization can you systematically improve your operations without creating chaos, and thereby gain adherence throughout the system when a better way is discovered.* Standard work itself is intended to provide a flexible and responsive workplace, where operators can move to the operations most needed to meet customer demand. Without standardization—adherence to the set standards—this orderly flexibility and responsiveness will be impossible to achieve.

Standardization and standard work benefit your company by reducing variability, waste, and costs. They help improve quality and shorten lead times and they lead the way to ISO certification. Standardization and standard work benefit you by making it easier for you to learn new operations, and easier for you to shift to different operations within a cell or move to other cells, lines, or work areas. They also provide the baseline for contributing new improvement ideas.

REFLECTIONS

Now that you have completed this chapter, take five minutes to think about these questions and to write down your answers:

- What did you learn from reading this chapter that stands out as particularly useful or interesting?

- Do you have any questions about the topics presented in this chapter? If so, what are they?

- What additional information do you need to fully understand the ideas presented in this chapter?

Chapter 2

Standardization

In Chapter 1 we define standardization as including the following three aspects:

1. The path to reliable methods

2. 100 percent adherence to reliable methods (through good communication)

3. Creating and maintaining improvements to standards

These all relate to the process of creating high-quality products at the lowest cost and in the shortest time. This chapter discusses these three elements of standardization in further detail.

The Path to Reliable Methods

Several sources of standards are mentioned in Chapter 1:

- Custom or consensus

- Scientific data or experience

- Technical specifications

The first two—custom and scientific data—refer to the change-able standards in production processes. The third—technical specifications—refers to the quality standards of the final product and rarely changes. A formula for establishing standards combines the process and technical standards as shown in Figure 2-1. In other words, standardization must incorporate both the product and the process standards to be effective in assuring the lowest cost, highest quality, and shortest delivery time for each product.

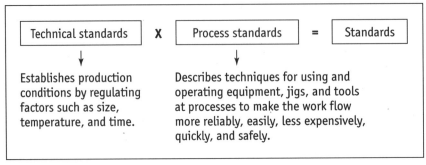

Figure 2-1. Formula for Establishing Standards

Types of In-House Standards

Figure 2-2 shows a list of eight types of in-house standards and the documents used in most plants to communicate them.

Type	Description
1. Regulations	These are formally established task management methods (job regulations, task regulations).
2. Quality standards	These are product quality requirements based on production standards specified by customers and adopted as in-house standards for products and inspection procedures.
3. Specifications	These are restrictions and other conditions placed on suppliers of equipment and parts. Usually, they are discussed and agreed on during supply contract negotiations.
4. Technical standards	These are the detailed standards concerning manufacturing methods and products. They stipulate dimensions, temperature, ingredients, strength characteristics, etc.
5. Process standards	These describe work procedures (processes). They usually appear in work procedure sheets or work instruction booklets.
6. Manuals	These are handbooks used for training and for detailed descriptions of work methods. They also define the company's standards and their objectives.
7. Circular notices	These notices inform people of new or revised standards, necessary preparations or responses, and other related matters.
8. Memos	Memos are a common means of communication for prior notification of extraordinary measures, temporary revisions, or other standard-related matters. They are also used for other types of notices, such as meeting minutes or in-house reports.

Figure 2-2. Types and Purposes of In-House Standards

100 Percent Adherence to Reliable Methods

Whether standards are process or product oriented, standardization depends on communication of the standard for 100 percent adherence to be achieved. Adherence to standards is the key to a strong improvement culture. *It is critical that you communicate the standards simply and easily so that everyone knows what they are and can follow them.*

Key Point

Communicating In-House Standards

Good standards manuals are hard to come by. Often the information in manuals is obscure and/or hard to find.

Manuals should include descriptions that are easy to understand, in language that conforms to the standards and conventions of each plant. All departments who need to refer to the same manuals should be able to understand them equally well. If different departments use different terms for the same things, all relevant terms should be included and defined. Standards formats should be adaptable so that only slight revisions to the manuals are required when product models or processes change. Information in manuals should be clearly oriented to its primary objective: maintaining high product quality and equipment performance.

Standards manuals should include only those items that must be adhered to by everyone. Those things that may be *preferred* by some do not belong in the manual. A good exercise for the plant would be to identify those items that must be adhered to and those that are optional, and then separate them. Do it twice. Think carefully about what must be done and narrow this list down to the minimum items that cannot be ignored. This will help your operators enormously to simplify the process of learning and checking while production is underway.

You can save time in updating changes if standards are kept in computer files. They can be easily accessed by anyone if they are stored as shared files. Items that do not need to be checked frequently can be moved to separate standards sheets or manuals. Items that need to be checked often should be positioned at each workstation in clear, easy-to-read formats, using as much visual information as possible.

Figure 2-3. Poor Communication of Standards

Manuals Are Often Not Designed for the User

Standards manuals typically are difficult to read, and therefore to follow. The organization of the material may not be clear or conform to the actual sequence that workers must follow. Therefore, information is difficult to find when it is needed. Checklisted items abound in manuals, but often their significance is unclear or unstated entirely. They may not be prioritized by importance or level of information, making it easy to overlook the most critical items. Standard procedure manuals may contain terms that are either too technical or too simplistic to be useful to the operator who needs the information to complete a process. Finally, manuals generally fail to describe how new hires can become veterans, making the information useless in building 100 percent adherence to the standards, the primary purpose of standardization itself.

Revisions Are Unsystematic

Manuals often remain unrevised for long periods of time even though the standards themselves have been changed and improved. Automated systems and error-proofing devices may have replaced obsolete checking procedures and data reporting methods described in older manuals. This creates confusion if workers do turn to manuals for clarification. What most often happens is that out-of-date manuals, which workers learn to ignore, become no more than weights using up space in work areas. Redundancy may exist between equipment manuals and quality control manuals; and discrepancies may exist between associates' notebooks and the information or language in the manuals. There may be no system for reviewing, evaluating, and revising the manuals, or manuals may be changed so frequently that they become unwieldy and confusing. Either way, this unsystematic approach to documenting standard procedures only leads to confusion and lack of standardization on the floor.

Information Is Not Consistent with Lean Production Methods

As lean production methods are established, inspection becomes part of every operation and cell. Since most operation manuals include checking and inspection points, redundancy occurs unless the manuals are revised as the new methods become standardized. Also, checkpoints are often added to the operating procedure to address uninvestigated causes of process difficulties. But if continuous improvement activities are well established, this should not occur.

Finally, standardization depends on procedures being fully described so that operators know what to do when problems arise. If values are outside control levels, standard procedures must tell the operator how to correct the variances. If machines cause defects, operators must know how to, and have the autonomy to, shut down the machine or the line to fix the problem. Empowerment must exist for each operator to check and correct any defects that may be produced, and to return any defects received from upstream so that no defects move downstream. Clear directions about what to do when standards are not followed or variances from standard occur are also part of the standardization process and must be clearly and visually displayed so that everyone is adequately informed.

TAKE FIVE

Take five minutes to think about these questions and to write down your answers:

1. What do you need to know? Who do you need to ask?
2. When and where do you need to know it?
3. What do you need to do so you have information when and where you need it?

Figure 2-4. Good Communication of Standards

What to Include in Standards Documentation

Technical and Process Standards Sheets

Example

Standards should be only one page, if possible, as in Figure 2-5, so that operators who need to refer to them can quickly see what is required. Technical and process standards should ideally include the following features:

1. Clear objectives of the standards.

2. Control points, checkpoints, and other management data—in both sentence form and symbols.

3. Checkpoints divided into categories of "must" versus "prefer," indicating both normal and abnormal ranges of operation.

4. Data charts that can be easily used during operations, using photos and drawings to show complex information.

Standards sheets should be posted at the work site. Color code the displays. Train employees in new standards so that 100 percent adherence can be achieved.

Equipment Manuals

Example

Equipment manuals should explain troubleshooting procedures, motion principles, and parts structures, as well as include parts service and supplier addresses. Standards manuals should include the following features:

1. Main title indicating the purpose of the manual.

2. Statement of scope or intended range of use.

3. Table of contents including titles of sections and subsections in each chapter.

4. Flowchart describing the information covered in the manual.

5. Section and subsection titles that name the central issues being discussed in the text.

6. Troubleshooting directions.

7. Equipment maintenance points and parts replacement and service periods. Addresses of suppliers should be located near this information.

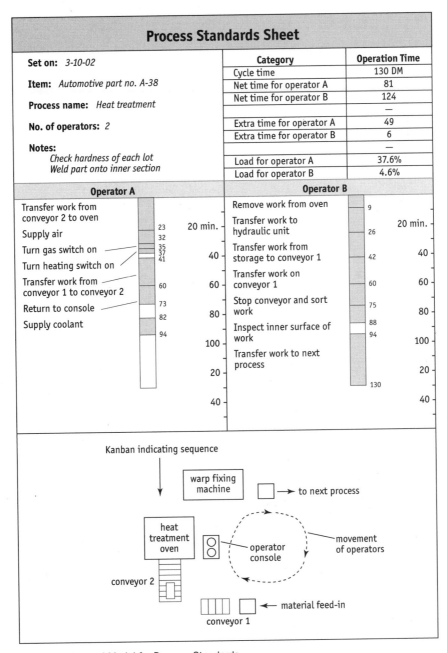

Process Standards Sheet

		Category	Operation Time
Set on: *3-10-02*		Cycle time	130 DM
		Net time for operator A	81
Item: *Automotive part no. A-38*		Net time for operator B	124
			—
Process name: *Heat treatment*		Extra time for operator A	49
No. of operators: *2*		Extra time for operator B	6
			—
Notes:		Load for operator A	37.6%
Check hardness of each lot		Load for operator B	4.6%
Weld part onto inner section			

Operator A

Transfer work from conveyor 2 to oven

Supply air

Turn gas switch on

Turn heating switch on

Transfer work from conveyor 1 to conveyor 2

Return to console

Supply coolant

23
32
35
37
41
60
73
82
94

20 min.
40
60
80
100
20
40

Operator B

Remove work from oven

Transfer work to hydraulic unit

Transfer work from storage to conveyor 1

Transfer work on conveyor 1

Stop conveyor and sort work

Inspect inner surface of work

Transfer work to next process

9
26
42
60
75
88
94
130

20 min.
40
60
80
100
20
40

Kanban indicating sequence

warp fixing machine

to next process

heat treatment oven

operator console

movement of operators

conveyor 2

conveyor 1

material feed-in

Figure 2-5. General Model for Process Standards

8. Examples of frequently asked questions and their answers.

9. A thorough alphabetical index.

10. Indication of authorization by the factory management, shown by stamp or initials.

The Value of User-Friendly Standards

When standards are communicated so that they are easy to find and use, many benefits result:

1. *Costs decrease:* fewer defective products are produced, overtime goes down, materials are not wasted.

2. *Delivery delays diminish:* equipment failures decrease, production operations become more reliable.

3. *Inspection costs disappear:* quality is built into each process, eliminating the need for inspection points downstream.

4. *Customer complaints decrease:* quality standards and delivery schedules are met consistently.

5. *Operations become more efficient and reliable:* anyone can easily learn the best way to produce quality products.

6. *Employee skills and morale increase:* the path from novice to veteran is easier and clearer and boosts enthusiasm, self-confidence, and skill.

Creating and Maintaining Improvements to Standards

The creation of standards and establishing standardization are important steps in any systematic continuous improvement activity. You must set up a spiral of improvement in standard operations that becomes an integral part of daily work. Figure 2-6 shows that first you must look at your current process and identify problems that exist. Search for the root cause of these problems. Solutions can then become part of the operating standard.

Example

An example will help clarify the power of following this improvement spiral carefully. In a particular plant newly hired operators are turning out a significant number of defects, while seasoned workers are producing no defects. It might seem that increased training is the solution, but a closer look is needed. In observing one of the workstations creating defects we learn that a veteran worker, who had had a zero defect rate, has just been transferred to another line and a new worker has replaced him. The machine he is in charge of taps bushings into the product. The reported defects, running at 5 percent since the new worker has run the machine, have damaged bush pins.

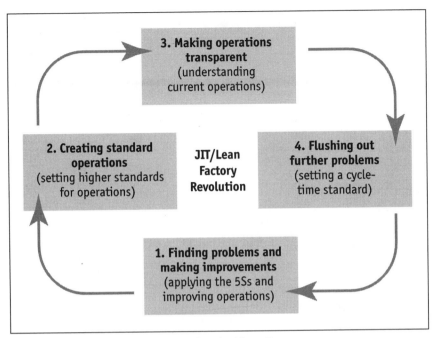

Figure 2-6. The Spiral of Improvement in Standard Operations

Several causes could exist: inexperience with the equipment, or idiosyncrasies in the equipment, or something else. We run a videotape to observe the two workers (the veteran and the new hire) doing the operation and we learn that the machine vibrates randomly, shifting the bush pin upward when placed on its corresponding part. The veteran worker knows this machine quirk and checks the bush pin each time. The new worker has not yet noticed this anomaly of the machine and defects are the result.

We can train the new operator to check the bush pin each time as the veteran has done, but does this solve the root cause? In the next chapter, one of the forms to be used in developing standard work is called a Standard Operations Pointers Chart. This can be used to communicate such unique occurrences in machines so that any operator coming to that workstation will be alerted to the idiosyncrasies that exist in that operation. However, this is not a question of worker error or lack of training, ultimately, but equipment defect. The solution to the *root cause* is to eliminate the vibration that causes the bush pin to shift out of position. Only by careful examination of what is going on can the root cause be discovered and eliminated.

TAKE FIVE

Take five minutes to think about these questions and to write down your answers:

1. Can you identify a problem in your work where more training will help resolve the issue?
2. Are there any problems in your work area that you have been avoiding by adding steps to your operation? Are these added steps documented? Have you discussed them with your improvement team?

How Do You Create Standards and Standard Operations?

The improvement example just given and the spiral depicted in Figure 2-6 are versions of the familiar Plan-Do-Check-Act cycle in total quality improvement. Standardization can easily be misunderstood if it is not recognized as just one recurring phase in this four-phase cycle. *Standardization is not only adherence to standards but also the continual creation of new and better standards.* Let's look more closely at this process to understand standardization more fully.

Key Point

Stages of Standards Improvement

How-to Steps

In Figure 2-7 a complete sequence for solving problems is shown. This is the *process* of standardization. Let's examine it step by step.

The first three steps in this process are involved in diagnosing the problem(s) you want to address. In Step 1 you identify and describe the problems. Problems exist in two forms, as shown in Figure 2-8:

- As variances from the established standard (Case 1)

- As variances between actual conditions and the projected future standard—the improvement goal (Case 2)

Refer again to Figure 2-7 as we continue through its steps. Organize the data you have gathered and determine the relative importance of solving each piece of data (Steps 2 and 3). Next choose the problem you want to address first and set a target for improvement (Steps 4 and 5). How will know when you have

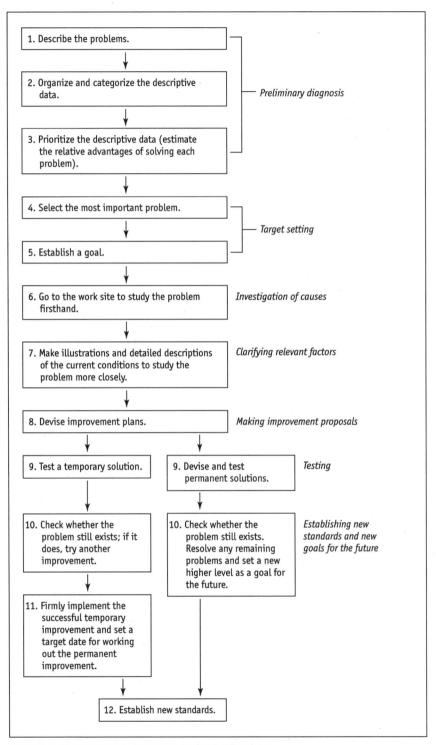

Figure 2-7. Standardization Sequence for Solving Problems

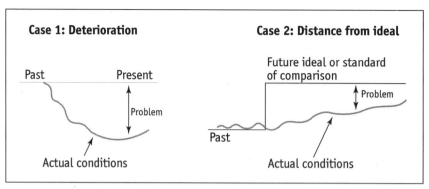

Figure 2-8. Two Forms of Problems and How They Occur

solved the problem? What measure will indicate this? In the bush pin example we gave, the target was a return to zero defects and this was achieved when the machine was repaired.

Next you investigate causes (Step 6). Use the Checklist for Finding the Facts at the Work Site (Figure 2-9) to find guidelines for discovering the root cause. A cause-and-effect diagram can be used to great advantage here. It is essential that you actually go to the work site and closely examine the operation or process being improved so that you do not make incorrect assumptions about the actual causes, which will cause you to solve the wrong problem, fail to find the *root cause*, and therefore have a return of the problem later or miss the real issues in some other way. You may want to ask an expert to help you identify what is going on to understand fully what you are addressing.

Once you have examined the problem carefully, draw and describe the current conditions in detail, and then brainstorm solutions (Steps 7 and 8 in Figure 2-7.) Once you have a number of solutions in mind, test some of them until you find the best one (Steps 9 through 11). After running the final solution through the process and checking that the problem is solved permanently, you are ready to establish this new standard and communicate it to everyone (Step 12).

1. *Determine causes:* Are there any defective products? If so, what are the causes? Study true characteristics, substitute characteristics, etc.

2. *Investigate variation:* Are the quality means values appropriate? Is the amount of variation appropriate?

3. *Classify:* Are there differences among groups? Classify by furnace, lot, job post, etc.

4. *Organize causes and effects:* If several problems are found, which are the most important? Learn to quickly draw up cause-and-effect lists that include at least 30 items.

5. *Analyze quantitatively:* How can the problems be described in quantitative terms? Which is the most frequent problem? Use Pareto analysis.

6. *Study variations in time series:* Taking current standards as the base, have you done a time-series analysis to look for variations that may indicate problems?

7. *Understand process links:* Does this process cause time-consuming problems at other processes? Does it create some other kind of problem for them? Does information flow smoothly among processes?

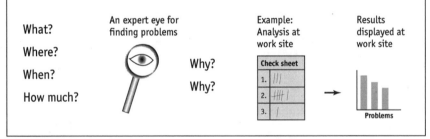

Figure 2-9. Checklist for Finding the Facts at the Work Site

An example of a Standard Operation Sheet is shown in Figure 2-10. Instructions for filling out this form are included in "Steps to Standard Work" in Chapter 3. It is shown here to give you an example of how to communicate the new standard so that 100 percent adherence can be attained. The detail is important if everyone is to understand exactly what the standard is. Examples of applications of standardization and examples of improvements to standard operations are given in Chapter 4. The reader can also review the references listed in Chapter 5 for more on applications of standardization.

Standard Operation Sheet

Issue date: _____

Approved by: (stamp)
Approved by: (stamp)

Operation:

Connect lead wires to snap terminal

Operation conditions:

Snap terminal is set in jig and lead wires are individually connected by hand

Technical standards:

1. Keep solder vat temperature at 220°C. Check daily using temperature gauge and controller.

2. Add flux to solder whenever the operation voucher specifies a lot change (use a scraper to remove slag build-up on solder surface).

3. Keep the flux vat at 80°C. The flux should be liquefied. Keep the flux level within the standard marks on the vat.

4. Use the stripper to remove the plastic sheaths from the lead wire. Check sample to measure exposed wire length (15mm). After stripping off the sheaths, bundle the wires to keep them together.

5. Always keep some solder on the soldering iron.

Materials:

1. Solder: H65S-W1.6
2. Snap terminal: Based on sample
3. Lead wires: Based on sample
4. Flux: 70°C melting point
                    (manufactured by A Co.)

Special notes:

1. The inspection consists of a tensile test on the soldered snap terminal (before cooling and before the plastic terminal has been screwed).

2. Be sure to describe any abnormal parts or operations and suggest improvement points.

Operation method diagram:

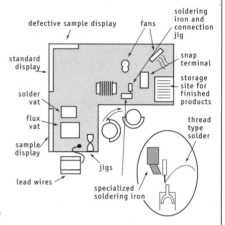

Operation steps: lot unit: 10 wires		
Steps	Time (sec.)	Points
1. Cut lead wires	15	Use cutter
2. Remove sheaths	20	Use stripper
3. Apply flux, then apply solder	30	Do one wire at a time and set wires in cooling jig when finished
4. Insert wire through plastic section	60	Set snap terrminal in jig
5. Solder and set down	60	Use specialized soldering iron
6. Move from jig to jig	15	Jig must cool down
7. Remove from jig and tighten screws	60	Do tensile strength test before assembly
Total	**330**	33 seconds per wire

Figure 2-10. Example of Standard Operation Sheet (for Soldering)

A Review of the Process Analysis Tools

Throughout the standardization improvement process you will
need to use quality control (QC) tools to analyze your data.
Figure 2-11 offers a review of these tools and shows at what stage
in the improvement process you are most likely to need them.

TAKE FIVE

Take five minutes to think about these questions and to write
down your answers:

1. What is the importance of going to the work site to study
   problems?
2. What must you do before establishing a new standard?

Standardization of operations goes hand-in-hand with equipment
improvement. Neither is more important than the other. The
example used in this chapter emphasized an equipment solution,
but the solution is more often than not found in the process
sequence or the waste in time and motion required by operators
when the process is not as good as it could be. Training is another
issue that sometimes solves the problem, but often it does not.
Every operator is skilled at accommodating to bad processes in
order to minimize their effects. It happens almost automatically.
The standardization process is designed to help you identify the
things you are doing to make up for problems in the process or the
equipment. By doing this you will be able to find permanent solutions to the aggravating and persistent difficulties you have been
facing every day. If you think of standards and standardization as
a one-time thing—fixed and never to be changed—then you will
miss the advantage of standardization as a continual learning and
improving mechanism for making your workday happier and easier. The improvement cycle becomes for many a meaningful and
rewarding part of everyday work. See Figure 2-12 for an image of
a satisfied worker focused on the standardization improvement
process. His legs represent the two actions—standardization and
equipment improvement—that move the improvement cycle
forward. One arm applies testing and verification and the other

Key Point

QC Tools	QC Steps									General use	Additional checkpoints for good ideas — alternative improvement methods
	Identify problems	Study current conditions (problem identification)	Infer causes	Check to verify causes	Brainstorm improvement plans	Evaluate and select improvement plans	Test improvement plans	Evaluate and verify effects	Standardize improvements		
1. Graphs	○	◎	○	○				◎	○	For gaining a temporal picture of changes and for making comparisons	Set standards and targets, then study causes of any deviation that occurs and make corrective improvement.
2. Histograms	○	◎						○		For understanding variations in data	Use the 5M categories to find the causes of variation. Then take the same approach described above.
3. Pareto diagrams	◎	○		○				○		For understanding which problems are most important	Use a check sheet along with the Pareto diagram. Take countermeasures that address the most significant problems.
4. Cause-and-effect diagrams			◎		○					For analyzing and identifying the causes of problems and suggesting methods of controlling them	Use the 5M categories and repeatedly ask "Why?" to gather facts while filling out the diagram.
5. Check sheets	○	○						○	◎	Facilitates the gathering and organization of data	Same as for Pareto diagrams.
6. Data stratification	◎	◎		◎				○		For grouping data to clarify differences	Set standard values, then investigate differences and their causes.
7. Scatter diagrams		○		◎						For studying targeted factors	Repeatedly ask "Why?" to clarify relationships among factors.
8. Control charts	○	○						○	◎	For understanding abnormal data trends	Study data trends as a time series to identify preventable causal factors.

◎ = Very useful   ○ = Useful

Figure 2-11. The Quality Control (QC) Tools and Their Uses

welcomes education and new technology to support improvement opportunities. His eyes are alert to visual standards and, along with his ears, process the continual upgrading of information. What he communicates is current, clear, and accurate. His consciousness is focused on target setting and problem solving. With this worker, the inflow of information and communication of new ideas is continual.

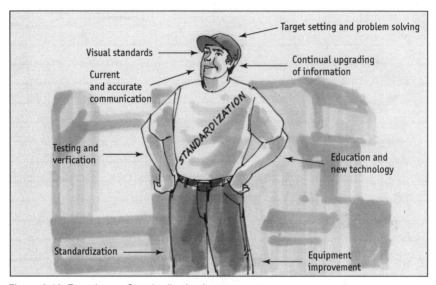

Figure 2-12. Focusing on Standardization Improvement

In Conclusion

SUMMARY

Standardization includes the following three aspects: the path to reliable methods; 100 percent adherence to reliable methods; and creating and maintaining improvements to standards. These all relate to the process of creating high-quality products at the lowest cost and in the shortest time.

Reliable methods result from custom or consensus, data derived from scientific methods, and technical specifications. The first two are changeable standards in production processes. The third refers to the quality standards of the final product and these rarely change.

Whether standards are process or product oriented, standardization depends on communication of the standard for 100 percent adherence to be achieved. Adherence to standards is the key to a strong improvement culture. *It is critical that you communicate the standards simply and easily so that everyone knows what they are and can follow them.* Good standards manuals are hard to come by. Often the information in manuals is obscure and/or hard to find. Manuals should include descriptions that are easy to understand, in language that conforms to the standards and conventions of each plant. Standards formats should be adaptable so that only slight revisions to the manuals are required when product models or processes change. Information in manuals should be clearly oriented to its primary objective: maintaining high product quality and equipment performance.

Standards manuals should include only those items that must be adhered to by everyone. Items that do not need to be checked frequently can be moved to separate standards sheets or manuals. Items that need to be checked often should be positioned at each workstation in clear, easy-to-read formats, using as much visual information as possible.

The creation of standards and establishing standardization are important steps in any systematic continuous improvement activity. You must set up a spiral of improvement in standard operations that becomes an integral part of daily work.

Standardization is not only adherence to standards but also the continual creation of new and better standards.

First you identify and describe the problem(s). Then you organize the data you have gathered and determine the relative advantage of solving each. Next choose the problem you want to address first and set a target for improvement, and then investigate causes. It is essential that you actually go to the work site and closely examine the operation or process being improved so that you do not make incorrect assumptions about the actual causes. Once you have examined the problem carefully, draw and describe the current conditions in detail, and then brainstorm solutions. Test some of them until you find the best one. After running the final solution through the process and checking that the problem is solved permanently, you are ready to establish this new standard and communicate it to everyone.

The standardization process is designed to help you identify the things you are doing to make up for problems in the process or the equipment. By doing this you will be able to find permanent solutions to the aggravating and persistent difficulties you have been facing every day. If you think of standards and standardization as a one-time thing—fixed and never to be changed—then you will miss the advantage of standardization as a continual learning and improving mechanism for making your workday happier and easier. The standardization improvement cycle can become a meaningful and rewarding part of your everyday work.

REFLECTIONS

Now that you have completed this chapter, take five minutes to think about these questions and to write down your answers:

- What did you learn from reading this chapter that stands out as particularly useful or interesting?

- Do you have any questions about the topics presented in this chapter? If so, what are they?

- What additional information do you need to fully understand the ideas presented in this chapter?

Chapter 3

Standard Work

Like all the lean production methods, standard work maximizes performance and minimizes waste. In Chapter 1, we said that standard work was a tool used to allocate worker and machine time in direct response to customer demand. *Standard work defines the most reliable work procedures and sequences for each process and operation so that operators can easily change positions within the process as needed to meet the current flow of orders.* Standard work describes the procedures and their sequences to support line balancing and full work, two aspects of pull production discussed in several other Shopfloor Series books as well as later in this chapter.

Key Point

Standard work involves three important elements shown in Figure 3-1:

1. Takt time

2. Standard work sequence

3. Standard work-in-process inventory

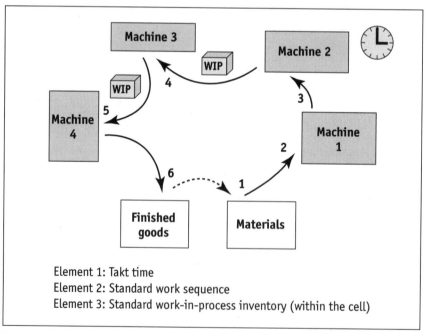

Element 1: Takt time
Element 2: Standard work sequence
Element 3: Standard work-in-process inventory (within the cell)

Figure 3-1. The Three Basic Elements of Standard Operations

Takt Time

Key Term

In a pull production system *takt time* is *the rhythm of production in harmony with the pulse of customer orders*. There are several terms used to describe and calculate the rate of production. They are often confused or misunderstood. Below are definitions and applications of the different terms to help you keep them straight.

Cycle Time

Key Term

Total cycle time is *the time from when the raw material enters a plant until a finished product is shipped*. If the cycle time of a complete process can be reduced to takt time, product can be made in one-piece flow. Continuous improvement in lean production works toward this goal.

Key Term

Key Terms

Operation cycle time is *the amount of time it takes one person to create one product within a cell or line*. Production output and operating time are the variables in calculating operation cycle time. If 20 parts are produced in an hour, cycle time for one operation is 3 minutes. *Operator cycle time* is *the total time it takes for an operator to complete one cycle of an operation (including walking, setup, inspection, etc)*. *Machine cycle time* is *the time from pressing "on" to when the machine returns to its original position after one operation cycle has been completed*. If a machine produces 60 parts each minute, its cycle time is one second.

Continuous improvement activities address cycle time as one of the most direct ways of eliminating waste. Improving cycle time means eliminating all extraneous, non-value-added activities until the operation is purely value-added, or as close to this as is possible. When the cycle time of an operation is free of waste the operation has become a reliable, standard method to be standardized throughout the factory. In a push system, cycle time is the speed at which you are able to produce product. In a pull system, cycle time is often used to mean end-of-line rate or takt time, which are defined next.

End-of-Line Rate

Key Term

End-of-line rate is the rate at which product comes off the production line. It is determined by dividing the units built per week by the plant production hours per week. The time increment of weeks will change to days or shifts as improvements are made until production is scheduled according to takt time. In a push system the end-of-line rate is determined according to predictions of demand. In a pull system end-of-line rate is based on actual customer demand; in this case end-of-line rate and takt time are two terms for the same thing.

Key Term

Takt time is the rate at which product must be turned out to meet customer demand; it is a calculated time that sets the pace of production to meet the flow of customer orders. To determine takt time, divide available production time by the rate of customer demand. If demand is 120 units per day and there are 480 minutes of operating time per day, then takt time is 4 minutes. If customers want only 4 products per month, takt time will be 1 week. *As you can see, this is not a measure of how many you are capable of producing but how many you must produce to meet demand.*

Key Point

Pitch is an adjustment of container amounts to takt time that allows work to flow more evenly on the shopfloor. It ensures that a manageable amount of "pack-out quantity" of the work in process is released to a downstream operation. Multiply takt time by pack-out quantity. If 20 units per container is the pack-out quantity and takt time is 1 minute, then pitch is 20 minutes—the time for a container to be produced and released to the next downstream cell, process, or operation.

End-of-line rate or takt time and pitch are recalculated whenever the number of hours available changes or there is a change in demand. Keeping the flow of production smooth, lines balanced, and takt time responsive to actual demand is the new challenge of production planning based on a pull system. The difficult task of predicting demand in a push system is replaced by the possibility of adjusting production daily, and ultimately shift-by-shift or even within a single shift, to meet the needs of a constantly changing customer environment.

TAKE FIVE

Take five minutes to think about these questions and to write down your answers:

1. What is the difference between cycle time and takt time? What is pitch?
2. Under what conditions are end-of-line rate and takt time the same?
3. When do you recalculate takt time?

Standard Work Sequence

Key Term

Key Point

Standard work sequence is the order of tasks involved in an operation or the order of operations in a process to complete an operation cycle. You should understand that *the process sequence and the work sequence may be different depending on the number of operators in a cell or on a line.* If takt time is slowed because of a decrease in customer demand for the product produced in that cell, then a single operator may be able to run all operations in the cell and keep up with the takt time. If demand increases, several operators may need to be moved into the cell to keep up with the accelerated takt time. In this case, the work sequence of each operator will be designed to keep individual cycle times down so that takt time can be met. Figure 3-2 shows a cell with two operators where one person operates stations 1, 2, 7, and 8 and the other operates stations 3, 4, 5, and 6. Standard work sequences should be created for every possible combination of workers in a given cell.

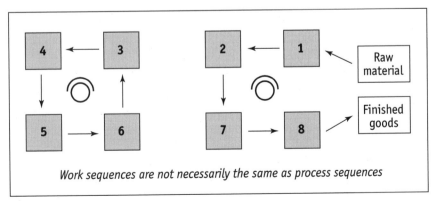

Work sequences are not necessarily the same as process sequences

Figure 3-2. Work Sequence vs. Process Sequence

Cell Staffing (Line Balancing and Full Work)

Key Term

Line balancing is *a calculation done to determine how many workers are needed on each line and in each cell to distribute work so that takt time can be met.* Line balancing insures that every worker will be used well, that idle time does not occur, and that some operators are not doing too much. This process to achieve full work has been defined clearly in many of the Shopfloor Series books and is summarized below and illustrated in Figure 3-3:

How-to Steps

1. Create a Process Map of the cell noting the current cycle times of each operation and create a Table of Current-State Data.

2. Create an Operator Balance Chart to represent the current-state data visually.

3. Determine the number of operators needed, using the following formula:

$$\text{\# of operators needed} = \frac{\text{Total cycle time}}{\text{Takt time}}$$

For example: $\dfrac{202 \text{ total cycle time}}{60 \text{ takt time}} = 3.36$

4. Add the desired-state data to the right side of the Operator Balance Chart.

At the current cycle times in this example, there is not quite enough work to keep four operators busy, but there is more than three can do. The desired state is to reduce cycle times so that three operators are sufficient—thus, improvement activities can address this goal. In the meantime, a part-time worker can complete the remaining parts required or the work can be moved to another cell where there may be an operator with time to spare.

Process Map for Line Balancing

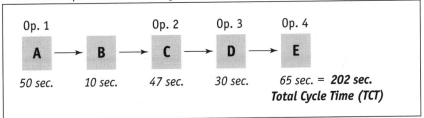

Table of Current-State Data

	Machine	Deburr	Crimp	Test	Mark
Cycle time	50 sec.	10 sec.	47 sec.	30 sec.	65 sec.
Changeover	60 min.	0	5 min.	5 min.	5 min.
Operators	1	0	1	1	1
Uptime	87%	100%	99%	99%	99%
Availability	27,600 sec.	27,600 sec.	27,600 sec.	27,600 sec.	27,600 sec.

Operator Balance Chart

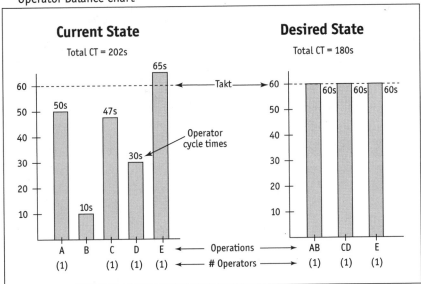

Figure 3-3. Steps to Balance the Line

Standard Work-in-Process Inventory (WIP)

Key Term

Standard work-in-process inventory is *the minimum amount of inventory that is needed for work to progress without creating idle time or interrupted production flow.* The Standard Operations Chart described later in this chapter is used to identify standard WIP inventories. The kanban system in pull production helps you reduce the amount of WIP to the minimum. Working with pitch and container capacities is another way of identifying and then reducing WIP. Continuous improvement of the standards in your process will allow you to reduce WIP to the minimum buffer, with the ideal goal always being "zero inventory."

TAKE FIVE

Take five minutes to think about these questions and to write down your answers:

1. If you experiment with your cell to determine the ideal work sequence for two operators versus three operators, what changes?

2. How many workers typically work in your cell? Does any station frequently have idle time? Is any station overworked or a bottleneck on a regular basis?

3. How much buffer stock do you usually have on hand for your cell or line?

Four Steps to Standard Work

How-to Steps

Step One: Create a Parts-Production Capacity Worktable

This worktable (Figure 3-4) describes the current capacity of each operation in the cell in terms of parts production. List the current processing capacity of each workstation on this form.

Fill out the worktable as follows:

a. Assign numbers to each operation in sequence and list them on the left of the worktable.

b. Enter the operation name and related machine number.

c. Enter the basic times for manual operation (A), auto feed or machine time (B), and completion time (C), which is the time to complete the operation (the sum of manual and machine times).

d. Then enter times for retooling (D, E, F).

e. Calculate totals for each operation (G).

f. Calculate totals of all operations at bottom and enter daily operating time (I).

g. The production capacity equals the result of dividing the total daily operating time (I) by the total time per unit (G).

h. Graph this time in the last column on the right of the table indicating manual time with a solid line (—) and machine time with a broken line (---). Indicate if manual time and machine time are:

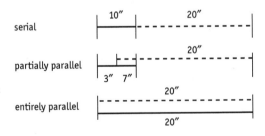

Parts-Production Capacity Worktable

Approval stamps:

Part #:	Type: RY	Entered by: Sato
Part name: 6" pinion	Quantity: 1	Creation date: 1/17/02

Sequence	Description of operation	Machine number	Basic times — Manual operation time (A) Min.	Sec.	Auto feed/ machine time (B) Min.	Sec.	Completion time (C)=A+B Min.	Sec.	Blades and bits — Retooling amount (D)	Retooling time (E)	Per unit retooling time (F)=E+D	Total time per unit (G)=C+F	Production capacity (I)(G)	Graph time (Manual work ——— / Auto feed ┄┄)
1	Pick up raw materials	—	1		—		1		—	—	—	1.0	—	
2	Gear teeth cutting	A01	4		35		39		400	2'10"	0.3"	39.3	717	4" 35"
3	Gear teeth surface fin.	A02	6		15		21		1,000	2'00"	0.1"	21.1	1,336	6" 15"
4	Foward gear surface fin.	A03	7		38		45		400	3'00"	0.5"	45.5	619	7" 38"
5	Reverse gear surface fin.	A04	5		28		33		400	2'30"	0.4"	33.4	844	5" 28"
6	Pin width measurement	B01	8		5		13		—	—		13.0	259	8" 5"
7	Store finished workpiece	—	1		—		1		—	—	—	1.0	—	8" 5"
	Total		32		2	1	2	33						Daily operating time (I): 7 hours, 50 min. = 28,200 seconds

Figure 3-4. A Sample Parts-Production Capacity Worktable

Step Two: Create a Standard Operations Combination Chart

The combination chart (Figure 3-5) takes the information from the Parts-Production Capacity Worktable and displays it visually by combining the manual and machine operations and showing their relationship in terms of process time. It includes setup time and walking time as well. Complete this chart as follows:

a. Draw a solid red line vertically on the graph to indicate the takt time. Remember, takt time is the available operating time divided by the required output (customer orders in the queue).

b. Calculate whether just just one worker can handle the cell or if more workers are needed. Using the Parts-Production Capacity Worktable, see if the sum of manual working time + walking time is less than the current takt time. Or refer to the process described earlier in the chapter for line balancing.

c. Enter the operation descriptions on the left in their sequence.

d. Enter the time measurements using a solid line for manual time, a broken line for machine time, and a wavy or diagonal line for walking time. Where manual and machine times are parallel, enter them as such.

e. Check the combination of operations. If machine time exceeds manual time then operators will be waiting for machine operations to be completed and the combination does not work as well as it should. If total time for all operations exceeds takt time, including walking back to the first operation to start a new cycle, then improvements may be made to shorten some of the cycle times, reduce walking time, etc. If total time falls short of takt time then perhaps additional operations can be added to the cell until takt time is achieved.

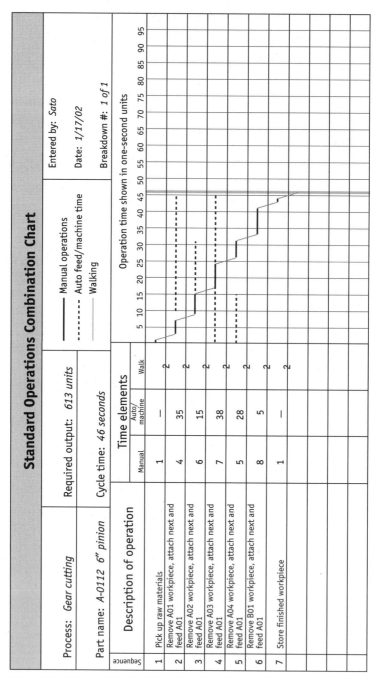

Figure 3-5. A Sample Standard Operations Combination Chart

Step Three: Create a Work Methods Chart

This chart details the process at each workstation, providing explicit instructions for new workers so that they will pick up the methods quickly and correctly.

Work Methods Chart							
Part #:		Required output:		Confirmation:		Name:	
Part name:		Breakdown name:		Dept:		Date:	
Cycle time:				Standard in-process inventory:			
Sequence	Description of operation	Quality		Critical factors (correct/incorrect, safety, facilitation, etc.)		Net time	
		Check	Measure			Min.	Sec.

Figure 3-6. A Sample Work Methods Chart

Step Four: Create a Standard Operations Chart (Standard Work Sheet)

The Standard Operations Chart provides an illustration of the process in a cell with the machine layout. It includes cycle time, work sequence, and standard work-in-process inventory, and includes any other information on standards in that cell. To ensure adherence to the standards, operators should check this chart frequently. Complete the Standard Operations Chart as follows:

a. Create a drawing of the machines as they are laid out in the cell or line and enter their work sequence number. Connect the machines with a solid line according to this sequence. Draw a broken line between the last and first step of the process.

b. Enter the quality checkpoints.

c. Enter the safety checkpoints.

d. Enter the WIP.

e. Enter the takt time and the net cycle time (including only the quality and safety checks or setups that are done for each cycle).

f. Enter the amount of standard WIP.

g. Enter the breakdown numbers to indicate different operators in the cell and total number of operators.

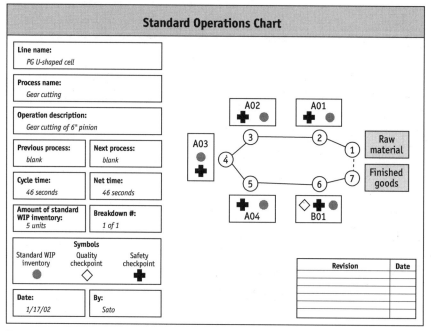

Figure 3-7. A Sample Standard Operations Chart

Additional Activities

Create a Visual Display of the Charts

The Standard Operations Combination Chart and the Standard Operations Chart can be joined to make a visual reference in the cell so that everyone can easily see the standards to be followed.

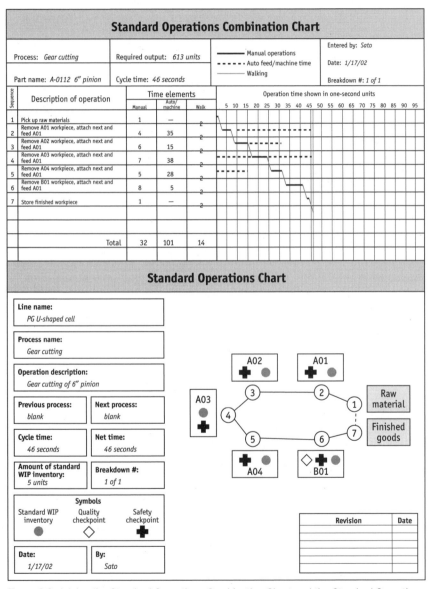

Figure 3-8. Joining the Standard Operations Combination Chart and the Standard Operations Chart for a Visual Display

Create a Standard Operations Pointers Chart

This chart is in a similar format to the Work Methods Chart and is used when there are important, unique guidelines needed for proper operation of particular equipment or when there are "handy hints" to the process that can be shared among operators at a given workstation. As these pointers accumulate you may take this chart to your improvement meeting to discuss possible additions to the standards, or ideas for making improvements in the process. Pointers may also indicate the need for new or different equipment, more frequent maintenance, and so on.

Standard Operations Pointers Chart			
Process name:	Department:		Confirmation:
Processing sequence:			
Machine #:	Date:		
Sequence	Description of operation	Critical factors (correct/incorrect, safety, facilitation, etc.)	Diagram of operation

Figure 3-9. A Sample Standard Operations Pointers Chart

TAKE FIVE

Take five minutes to think about these questions and to write down your answers:

1. What is the relationship between the Parts-Production Capacity Worktable and the Standard Operations Combination Chart?

2. How does the Standard Operations Chart help you standardize your process?

Improvement of Operations for Standard Work

Improvements in standard work can be focused on many aspects of production operations.

1. Improvements to the flow of materials

2. Shifting from specialization to multi-skilled lines and operators

3. Improvements in motion

4. Establishing rules for operations

5. Improvements in equipment

6. Separation of people and machines

7. Preventing defects

The flow of materials is greatly improved by implementing cell design, changing from specialized operations where all machines of one type are placed together to placing equipment in the sequence it is used to complete an operation or process. See Figure 3-13 for an example of a cellular layout. Multi-skilled workers support this cellular layout, making it possible to balance the number of workers on a line or in a cell in response to customer demand. See the Shopfloor Series books on cell design and pull production, listed in Chapter 5, for detailed information on how to implement these improvements.

Improvements in operation motions can be achieved by focusing on several aspects of an operation.

1. Placement of parts—See Figure 3-10 for an example of this.

2. Picking up parts—See Figure 3-11 for an example of this.

3. Shifting from one-handed to two-handed tasks—See Figure 3-12 for an example of this.

4. Elimination of walking waste—See Figure 3-13 for an example of this.

Key Point

Improvements in motion are among the most important changes that can be made in the standardization process. They improve every operator's efficiency and effectiveness. Also, searching for ways to improve one's own operation by reducing motion empowers everyone to participate and improve their own work conditions. This a powerful aspect of the standardization process and cannot be emphasized enough in creating standard work procedures. It is the basis for establishing rules for operations that *make sense* and will be followed by everyone.

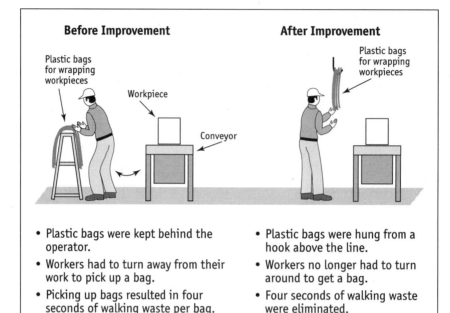

Figure 3-10. Improvement in the Placement of Parts

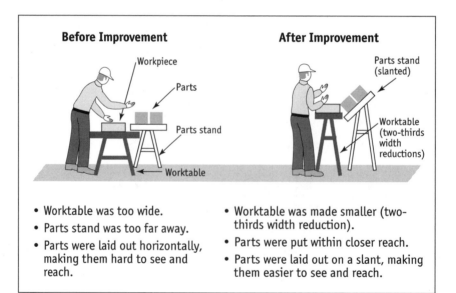

Figure 3-11. Improvement in Picking Up Parts

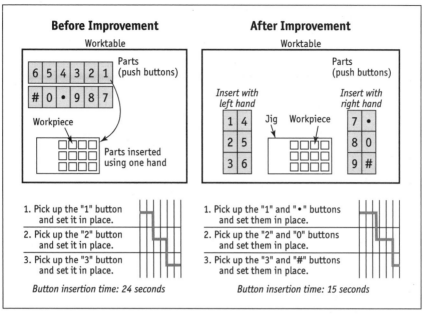

Figure 3-12. Shifting from One-Handed to Two-Handed Tasks

These and all the other focuses for improvement are integral to the process of creating and continually improving standard work methods. Refer to the other books in the Shopfloor Series for ways to improve standard operations.

TAKE FIVE

Take five minutes to think about these questions and to write down your answers:

1. How much time do you spend looking for materials or tools to do your work?

2. How many miles do you walk in a day just to do your work? (This does not mean distance to lunch or breaks, but actual operation time spent walking.) Put on a pedometer and find out.

3. Can you think of one change you could make to reduce this distance by half?

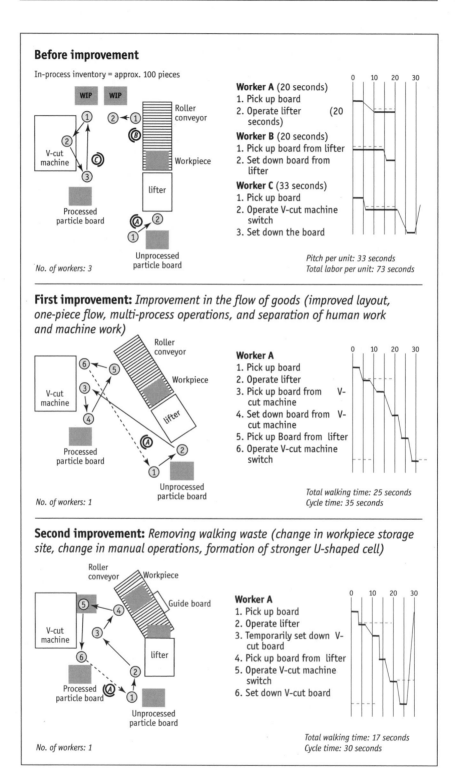

Before improvement

In-process inventory = approx. 100 pieces

WIP   WIP

Roller conveyor

V-cut machine

Workpiece

Processed particle board

lifter

Unprocessed particle board

No. of workers: 3

Worker A (20 seconds)
1. Pick up board
2. Operate lifter   (20 seconds)

Worker B (20 seconds)
1. Pick up board from lifter
2. Set down board from lifter

Worker C (33 seconds)
1. Pick up board
2. Operate V-cut machine switch
3. Set down the board

0   10   20   30

Pitch per unit: 33 seconds
Total labor per unit: 73 seconds

First improvement: *Improvement in the flow of goods (improved layout, one-piece flow, multi-process operations, and separation of human work and machine work)*

Roller conveyor

Workpiece

V-cut machine

lifter

Processed particle board

Unprocessed particle board

No. of workers: 1

Worker A
1. Pick up board
2. Operate lifter
3. Pick up board from V-cut machine
4. Set down board from V-cut machine
5. Pick up Board from lifter
6. Operate V-cut machine switch

0   10   20   30

Total walking time: 25 seconds
Cycle time: 35 seconds

Second improvement: *Removing walking waste (change in workpiece storage site, change in manual operations, formation of stronger U-shaped cell)*

Roller conveyor

Workpiece

Guide board

V-cut machine

lifter

Processed particle board

Unprocessed particle board

No. of workers: 1

Worker A
1. Pick up board
2. Operate lifter
3. Temporarily set down V-cut board
4. Pick up board from lifter
5. Operate V-cut machine switch
6. Set down V-cut board

0   10   20   30

Total walking time: 17 seconds
Cycle time: 30 seconds

Figure 3-13. Improvement in the Flow of Goods and Walking Time in Cabinet Processing

54

Ten Guidelines for Maintaining Standard Work

The following are some effective guidelines for maintaining standard work.

1. Establish standard operations universally throughout the factory, which are completely supported by top management.

2. Make sure everyone understands the importance of standard operations—from the president to the newest employee.

3. See that workshop leaders and anyone responsible for training others in standard operations are confident in and committed to the standard operations they teach.

4. Post visual displays to remind everyone of the importance of adhering to the standards.

5. Post graphic and text descriptions of the standard operations so that workers can compare their own work to the standards.

6. Bring in a third party to clear up any misunderstandings.

7. Hold workshop leaders responsible for maintaining standard work.

8. Reject the status quo. Remember that improvement never ends, and continually look for ways to improve the existing standards.

9. Conduct small-group improvement activities regularly to gather new ideas and alert one another to problems as they arise.

10. Systematically pursue the establishment of a new, higher level of standard work.

In Conclusion

SUMMARY

Like all the lean production methods, standard work maximizes performance and minimizes waste. *Standard work defines the most reliable work procedures and sequences for each process and operation so that operators can easily change positions within the process as needed to meet the current flow of orders.* Standard work involves three important elements: takt time, standard work sequence, and standard work-in-process inventory.

In a pull production system *takt time* is *the rhythm of production in harmony with the pulse of customer orders.* There are several terms used to describe and calculate the rate of production that are important to understand. These include *total cycle time, operation cycle time, operator cycle time, machine cycle time, end-of-line rate, takt time,* and *pitch.*

Standard work sequence is *the order of tasks involved in an operation or the order of operations in a process to complete an operation cycle.* You should understand that *the process sequence and the work sequence may be different depending on the number of operators in a cell or on a line.* If takt time is slowed because of a decrease in customer demand for the product produced in that cell, then a single operator may be able to run all operations in the cell and keep up with the takt time. If demand increases, several operators may need to be moved into the cell to keep up with the accelerated takt time. *Line balancing* is *a calculation done to determine how many workers are needed on each line and in each cell to distribute work so that takt time can be met.*

Standard work-in-process inventory is *the minimum amount of inventory that is needed for work to progress without creating idle time or interrupted production flow.* The kanban system in pull production helps you reduce the amount of WIP to the minimum.

There are four steps to achieving standard work:

    Step One. Create a Parts-Production Capacity Worktable

    Step Two. Create a Standard Operations Combination Chart

Step Three. Create a Work Methods Chart

Step Four. Create a Standard Operations Chart

You can also create a visual display of the forms by joining the Standard Operations Combination Chart and the Standard Operations Chart so that everyone can easily see the standards to be followed.

Improvements in standard work can be focused on many aspects of production operations. *Improvements in motion are among the most important changes that can be made in the standardization process.*

There are important guidelines for maintaining standard work. It is critical in establishing standard operations that they be universally applied throughout the factory and completely supported by top management. Make sure everyone understands the importance of standard operations—from the president to the newest employee. Post visual displays to remind everyone of the importance of adhering to the standards, and systematically pursue the establishment of a new, higher level of standard work.

REFLECTIONS

Now that you have completed this chapter, take five minutes to think about these questions and to write down your answers:

- What did you learn from reading this chapter that stands out as particularly useful or interesting?

- Do you have any questions about the topics presented in this chapter? If so, what are they?

- What additional information do you need to fully understand the ideas presented in this chapter?

Chapter 4

Applications of Standardization and Standard Work

Applications of Standardization

In Chapter 2, standardization was defined and ways to communicate standards were described in some detail. The process of improving and setting new standards was also described. In this chapter we offer a number of specific applications of standardization to help you identify improvement targets for specific purposes.

New Employee Training

There are three types of training standards to be considered:

1. Employee-to-employee training

2. Training by specialists or managers

3. Training by visual management

Guidelines for these follow.

Employee-to-employee training: This is usually on-the-job training and is the most common system of training used in factories. However, to be effective it requires standardization and the scrutiny of continuous improvement cycles to support adherence to reliable methods. Guidelines are listed below for what happens in effective employee-to-employee training.

1. The teaching employee discusses the importance of the operation.

2. Basic points of the operation are covered.

3. Safety concerns are described.

4. A slow demonstration of each step of the operation is given, with an explanation of how to make the work easier, quicker, and more reliable.

5. After watching the operation performed, the trainee describes it, and then attempts it under supervision. Begin with the easier steps until they are perfected, then move to the more complex steps of the operation.

6. The trainee performs the operation unassisted, with occasional review by the teaching employee when mistakes are made.

7. The new employee is welcomed into the group and invited to the improvement activities, and perhaps assigned a special problem-solving task.

APPLICATIONS OF STANDARDIZATION AND STANDARD WORK

Training by specialists or managers: Specialists or managers follow similar guidelines for training employees as in employee-to-employee training. The training should always be hands-on at the worksite, even if fundamentals are covered in a classroom. After mastering the basics, teachers should make sure trainees understand the relevant troubleshooting methods.

Posting the training that each operator has completed is a good way that trainers can reward and encourage employees to learn more skills. See Figure 4-1. In lean production, operators are responsible for multiple operations within one cell. They may also be moved from cell to cell as customer demand changes production needs and line balancing shifts their responsibilities. This aspect of lean production requires union support. Multi-tasking creates an environment where operators are encouraged to expand their skills training.

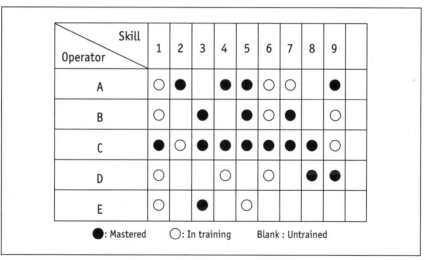

Figure 4-1. Skills Achievement Chart

Training by visual management: Visual displays of targets and measures, differences between standards and actual results, and the standard work methods themselves, give significant feedback on how well operations are adhering to the standards. These displays are posted at workstations and in cells and work areas so that operators can use them to correct variances and recognize where problems exist. Different uses of visual management aids are listed in Figure 4-2.

Management Target	Implementation Items
1. Process management and deadline management	Production management board (for progress control), fluid curve chart (a graph comparing target values to result values), display boards (e.g., for work instructions, parts delivery schedules, and urgent items or delayed deliveries).
2. Quality control	Defect graph (rate and trends), defective goods storage area, display of defect-prevention rules, defect samples, etc.

3. Operation management	Operating status display lamps:
	  Green = normal condition
	  Yellow = changeover in progress
	  Red = breakdown or abnormality
	Operation standards (technical standards and process standards), multiskills training achievement chart, cutting tool replacement schedule and results chart, and equipment capacity utilization graph; bulletin boards for notices regarding causes of minor line stoppages, improvement campaign results, etc.

4. Materials and parts management	Storage site specifications, part names, kanban card displays, displays of minimum and maximum allowable inventory, floor area and height restrictions for storage areas; defect storage site indicators; notices about missing inventory items, retained items, items awaiting disposal, items to be repaired, etc.
5. Management of equipment, jigs, and tools	Maintenance schedules and results charts; displays of equipment checkpoints (sections and check items); routine inspection check sheets; storage site instructions for dies, jigs, and tools (including inventory and ordering information); spare parts inventory; inventory shelf management; tags indicating name of equipment manager; notices describing reasons for breakdowns; etc.
6. Safety	Safety guidelines and special safety-related notices.
7. Improvement goals and improvement management	Weekly and daily charts showing progress toward improvement targets, equipment capacity utilization results, defect elimination results, work-in-process and warehouse imventory trend charts, safety trend charts, 5S and PM activity progress charts, improvement proposal campaign results, displays of improvement case studies, etc.

Figure 4-2. Examples of Visual Management Targets and Implementation Items

---

TAKE FIVE

Take five minutes to think about these questions and to write down your answers:

1. What type of on-the-job training do you have at your plant? Is top management involved in the training process?
2. Do you have support for multi-skill training?
3. What types of visual displays do you have for communicating standards in your plant?

Quality Design

Quality means zero defects in the product produced. But since "second-rate" products can be produced perfectly, we need to consider what else quality can mean. First, a quality product should satisfy customer needs in some way. Second, the product should be reliable—it should work without breakdowns, be easy to use, and be easy to maintain and repair. And it doesn't hurt if it's attractive. The way customers use a product should determine the specific quality features built into it.

There are a number of factors to consider when appraising the quality of products. Standardized methods can be applied to this appraisal. Figure 4-3 shows how eleven product features were first prioritized in order of importance to the customer and then placed in a grid according to the type of quality factor each represented. In this example, by making sure that the first seven features are designed into the product, all four quality aspects will be addressed.

Basic quality factors		Factors that distinguish the product from the competition	
1. Basic functions 2. No negative effects 5. Safety		3. Running costs 11. Durability	*Example:* Product with distinctive technology
4. Operability 6. Maintainability 10. Versatility	*Example:* Daily-use products	7. Ease of installation 8. Enjoyability 9. Attractiveness	*Example:* Designer products
Secondary (bonus) quality factors		**Factors that enhance marketability**	

Figure 4-3. Product Quality Appraisal Factors and Their Significance

See the reference section at the end of this book for quality function deployment (QFD) and other methods to improve design quality to meet customer needs and reduce production costs as well.

Evaluating Improvement Ideas

Key Point

The process of creating standards must also be standardized for effective standards to be developed and followed. In Chapter 2, this process was discussed in detail. One additional aspect of the improvement process worth mentioning here is the method of generating and evaluating new ideas.

There are always a number of ways to solve problems and many improvement plans will emerge as teams begin to analyze their operations. How should they choose the ones to standardize?

First, make sure that all ideas are collected. Figure 4-4 shows an Idea Sheet, which can be used to track and illustrate ideas as they

Objectives	Ideas	Plan Illustration
1. Attach flux to parent material	1. Use resinous solder 2. Apply flux by hand 3. Apply molten flux to wire	**Plan A:** Improvement in manual operation (1.1) + (2.1) + (3.5) ... resinous solder — soldering iron — wire — stabilizing jig made of heat-resistant material
2. Attach solder to parent material	1. Apply well-soldered iron tip to parent material 2. Apply molten solder to wire 3. Insert solder between wire and parent material; apply heat quickly to melt the solder	**Plan B:** Preheating method (1.3) + (2.2) + (3.1) ... 1. Dip wire in molten flux 2. Dip wire in molten solder 3. Apply soldering iron Preheating jig
3. Heat parent material	1. Use heater for preheating 2. Heat parent material to solder melting point 3. Preheat flux to melting point	**Plan C:** Spot welding method (1.3) + (2.3) + ...

Note: Numbers in parentheses are combinations of ideas from each of the objectives.

Figure 4-4. Idea Sheet

arise in an operator's mind. If all ideas for solving a particular problem are written down and then illustrated it will be easier for the team to understand the solutions being presented and discuss their value. In Figure 4-5, the Idea Evaluation Chart, the team goes one step further and evaluates each idea based on technical merit, cost savings, and operator use. At this point it should be easy to identify the best solution and implement it.

Idea	Primary Evaluation Criteria			Conclusion
	Technical	Operator-related (including safety)	Economic (including operating costs)	
Plan A: Improvement in manual operation 1. Use resinous solder 2. Apply a large amount of solder to the solder iron tip, then apply solder 3. Use a specialized jig to stabilize the plug	◎ Feasible even under current conditions	△ Requires veteran skills; training will be needed	◎ Inexpensive: only solder material needs changing	○ Try using the specialized jig, give verbal instructions
Plan B: Preheating method 1. Apply flux beforehand 2. Dip wire into molten solder 3. Set plug into preheating device	◎ Requires only a new jig	◎ Can be done by setting standard sequence	○ Jig improvement can be done inexpensively	◎ Implement and write new standard sheet
Plan C: Spot welding method 1. Apply flux to wire 2. Apply wire to spot welder tip and insert solder for quick melting	○ Requires tests for technical problems (test new materials, etc.)	◎ Easy to do	△ Spot welder investment required: about $77,000	△ Postpone

Merit: △ = weak ○ = medium ◎ = strong

Figure 4-5. Idea Evaluation Chart

TAKE FIVE

Take five minutes to think about these questions and to write down your answers:

1. What are some factors involved in creating quality product designs?

2. How do you keep track of ideas now for solving problems in your plant? Do you have a method for evaluating which ones are best?

Production Management

Production management aims to control the production variables—what, when, where, and how many activities it takes to deliver products of the highest quality, in the shortest time, and for the lowest costs. It helps smooth the flow of activities from the customer order to its delivery. Production management can serve a number of purposes, all of which are related to the type of customer and the customer needs being served by a product or service. Figure 4-6 shows the functions of production management and how to create checkpoints according to the Plan-Do-Check cycle of continuous improvement. It breaks down the management functions into three aspects: planning, implementing, and supervision.

Key Point

In the standardization of production management, the methods of lean production create visual checkpoints throughout the production process for all aspects of the management function so that communication is immediate and universal. Heijunka boxes communicate the demand and regulate the flow of production and/or the flow of material withdrawal and use. Kanban cards communicate the demand upstream, ultimately determining raw material ordering and regulating supplier relationships. Visual displays and controls, error-proofing, and quick changeover methods continually decrease work-in-process inventory and defects. *Operators become their own inspectors of both the process and the technical standards.*

The ultimate end of lean production is the ability to implement a production system with a high degree of flexibility to respond to changes in customer demand. This is discussed in the last section of this chapter on small lots and level loads.

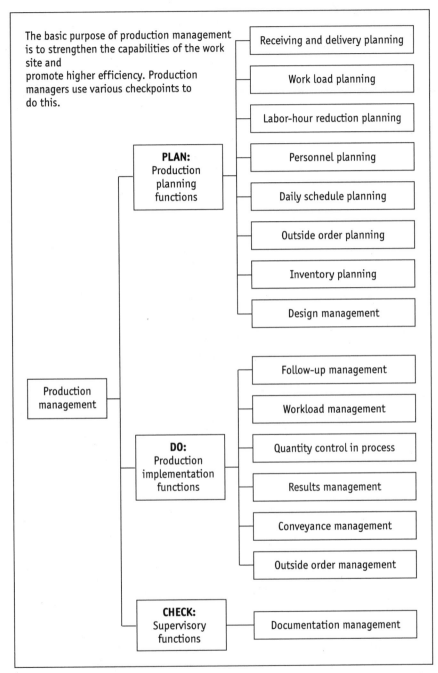

The basic purpose of production management is to strengthen the capabilities of the work site and promote higher efficiency. Production managers use various checkpoints to do this.

Production management

PLAN: Production planning functions
- Receiving and delivery planning
- Work load planning
- Labor-hour reduction planning
- Personnel planning
- Daily schedule planning
- Outside order planning
- Inventory planning
- Design management

DO: Production implementation functions
- Follow-up management
- Workload management
- Quantity control in process
- Results management
- Conveyance management
- Outside order management

CHECK: Supervisory functions
- Documentation management

Figure 4-6. Production Management Functions

Decision-Making

When standards exist, a manager's responsibility becomes easier because everyone knows what to do and how to do it. *Standards support the delegation of responsibility.* Figure 4-7 shows a diagram of the relationship between the standards and the chain of responsibility.

TAKE FIVE

Take five minutes to think about these questions and to write down your answers:

1. What are a few functions of the production management role?
2. How does lean production simplify production management?

Applications of Standard Work

At the beginning of this book we say that standard work is the culmination of lean production. Hopefully, by now, you understand why. Standards are the foundation of continuous improvement. Without them you cannot focus or measure your improvements. By the time you have implemented a cell layout, quick changeover, and standard work, everyone should have embraced a culture of continuous improvement. Standards and standard work, as we have shown throughout this book, are not static or unchanging. In fact, they are the basis from which improvement changes can be analyzed and tested and then adopted by everyone systematically. They are the content of training efforts—you train people to adhere to both technical and process standards. Standard work, when implemented, creates an even workload for every operator, so that no one works too little or too much, idle time is reduced, and bottlenecks are eliminated. Balanced lines and standard work procedures are the basis for small-lot, level-load production—the ultimate key to customer satisfaction and reduced costs.

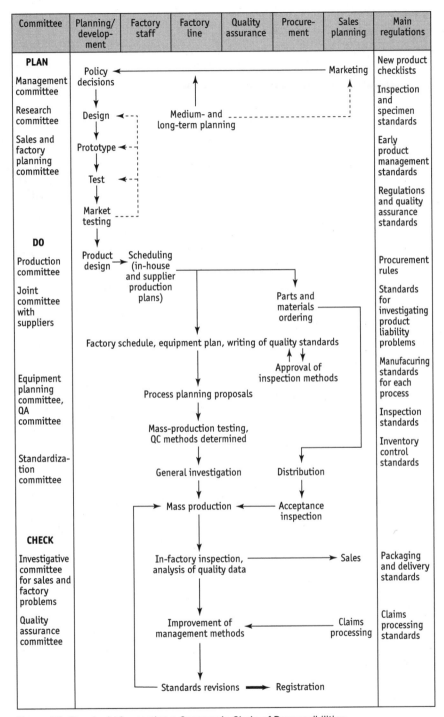

Committee	Planning/ development	Factory staff	Factory line	Quality assurance	Procure- ment	Sales planning	Main regulations
PLAN Management committee Research committee Sales and factory planning committee	Policy decisions Design Prototype Test Market testing		Medium- and long-term planning			Marketing	New product checklists Inspection and specimen standards Early product management standards Regulations and quality assurance standards
DO Production committee Joint committee with suppliers Equipment planning committee, QA committee Standardiza- tion committee	Product design	Scheduling (in-house and supplier production plans) Factory schedule, equipment plan, writing of quality standards Process planning proposals Mass-production testing, QC methods determined General investigation Mass production	Parts and materials ordering Approval of inspection methods Distribution Acceptance inspection			Procurement rules Standards for investigating product liability problems Manufacuring standards for each process Inspection standards Inventory control standards
CHECK Investigative committee for sales and factory problems Quality assurance committee		In-factory inspection, analysis of quality data Improvement of management methods Standards revisions ➡ Registration			Sales Claims processing	Packaging and delivery standards Claims processing standards

Figure 4-7. Standards Supporting a Company's Chain of Responsibilities

Production Management for Small Lots and Level Loads

Key Point

In order to set up a pull system using kanban and/or small-lot production using load leveling, standard work is necessary. Without (1) standards in place, (2) standardization which is functioning as part of daily work, and (3) standard work determining the process sequence and allowing balanced lines, small-lot production and load leveling will not be possible. Fluctuations in demand, last-minute changes to a customer order, and rush orders can only be fulfilled if flexibility in the production process is a reality. When you can move operators from cell to cell because they are multi-skilled and trained in the standard operations of each work station, when you have standard work sequences visually displayed no matter how many operators are working a cell, and when you have load-leveling that allows you to produce small lots and change the order of production to respond to last-minute changes in demand, then you have achieved lean production. Costs will be at a minimum, quality will be at a maximum, delivery will be on time in the shortest time—and all of these will be the baselines driving further improvements in each.

Figure 4-8 shows the results of a production system when it switches to small-lot, level production. Notice the difference in average work-in-process to achieve the same results. Also note that if any last-minute changes are made in quantity or features for any model, these can be accommodated before the week is out because all models are being made each day. Quick changeover is obviously a critical component for achieving this flexibility.

In Figure 4-9, three types of production requirements are shown, all implementing flow conditions. Different factories require different systems. Highly repetitive production is best served using kanban and pull production. Job shops with one-time production instructions can implement one-piece flow to advantage. Wide variety production shops with both upstream and downstream instructions can still adjust work-in-process to achieve leveled production. All can use kanban or a modified kanban system to allow downstream changes to be built into production orders and load leveling to be achieved.

Production conditions
- Production output: 1,000 units per day.
- Line enables mixed production of up to three different product models.
- Line operates on one eight-hour shift per day, thirty days per month.

Previous production system

Model	Request from downstream processes	Day 1	Day 2	Day 3	Day 4	Day 5	Output/ month	Total productions days	Average work-in process
A	400 units/day	1,000			1,000		12,000	12	1,500
B	200		1,000				6,000	6	900
C	400			1,000		1,000	12,000	12	1,600
---	1,000	1,000	1,000	1,000	1,000	1,000	30,000	30	4,000

New small-lot quick-changeover production system (leveled production)

Model	Request from downstream processes	Day 1	Day 2	Day 3	Day 4	Day 5	Output/ month	Total productions days	Average work-in process
A	400	400	400	400	400	400	12,000	12	500
B	200	200	200	200	200	200	6,000	6	300
C	400	400	400	400	400	400	12,000	12	500
---	1,000	1,000	1,000	1,000	1,000	1,000	30,000	30	1,300

Advantages of new production system
- It can respond easily to variation in product output.
- It has a shorter lead time, less inventory, and makes better use of available space.
- It provides daily feedback of quality information.

Figure 4-8. Establishing Small-Lot Level Production

Type	Kanban system	Upstream & downstream process instructions	Job shop (one-time) instruction
Suitable use	Highly repetitive production (values + 10%)	Nonrepetitive production (varies widely)	One-piece production (per order production)
Instructions and flow of goods	Daily schedule instructions — Process WIP — Kanban instructions: *Number of kanban Lot size per kanban Total lot size*	Feed-in instructions Manufacturing instructions — Adjusted while monitoring WIP	Feed-in and manufacturing instructions — Status management — One-time instructions

Figure 4-9. Flow Production in Three Types of Systems

TAKE FIVE

Take five minutes to think about these questions and to write down your answers:

1. What are some advantages to small-lot, level production?
2. How does standard work support small-lot, level production?
3. What type of production is done at your shop—highly repetitive or nonrepetitive?

Satisfied Employees

Generally, you will discover that everyone resists standardization until they understand what it really means and how it benefits the company and workers alike. It is often thought that standard procedures will destroy innovation and creativity. People don't want to do it the same way as everyone else, and they don't want to do it the same way every time. It seems boring. But in fact, *100 percent of the time, once standardization is in effect and standard work is in place, creativity, improvement, and job satisfaction increase.* There is now a system that is part of daily work to test and improve the standards. Recognition for making improvements builds self-esteem, and skill levels are increased through training for multi-skill work. Conditions for boredom and resentment—idle time and overwork—are eliminated. Training

Key Point

becomes more effective, turnover rate drops, communication among teams and between shifts is increased—people know what they need to know when they need to know it. Only after working in an environment where standard work is in place do you discover the advantages to each operator that inevitably result.

Standardization and standard work procedures depend on and derive from all the methods of the lean production system; they bring these methods to their full potential; and they set in motion a continuous improvement cycle for the whole plant that is never ending.

In Conclusion

SUMMARY

In this chapter we offer a number of specific applications of standardization to help you identify improvement targets for specific purposes: new employee training, quality design, evaluating improvement ideas, production management, and decision-making.

New employee training includes employee-to-employee training, training by specialists or managers, and training by visual management. Employee-to-employee, on-the-job training is the most common system of training used in factories. However, to be effective it requires standardization and the scrutiny of continuous improvement cycles to support adherence to reliable methods. Training by specialists or managers should always be hands-on at the worksite, even if fundamentals are covered in a classroom. After mastering the basics, teachers should make sure trainees understand the relevant troubleshooting methods. Training by visual management uses displays of targets and measures, differences between standards and actual results, and the standard work procedures themselves to give feedback on how well operations are adhering to the standards. These displays are posted at workstations and in cells and work areas so that operators can use them to correct variances and recognize where problems exist.

Quality design ensures zero defects in the product produced. But since second-rate products can be produced perfectly, we need to consider what else quality means. First, a quality product should satisfy customer needs in some way. Second, the product should be reliable—it should work without breakdowns, be easy to use, and be easy to maintain and repair. It doesn't hurt if it's attractive. The way customers use a product should determine the quality features built into it.

Evaluating improvement ideas and *the process of creating standards must also be standardized for effective standards to be developed and followed.* There are always a number of ways to solve problems and many improvement plans will emerge as teams begin to analyze their operations. How should they choose the ones to standardize? First, make sure that all ideas are collected. If all ideas for solving a particular problem are written down and then illustrated it will be easier for the team to understand the solutions being presented and discuss their value. The team then goes one step further and evaluates each idea based on technical merit, cost savings, and operator use. At this point it should be easy to identify the best solution and implement it.

Production management aims to control the production variables—what, when, where, and how many activities it takes to deliver products of the highest quality, in the shortest time, and for the lowest costs. It helps smooth the flow of activities from the customer order to its delivery. Production management can serve a number of purposes, all of which are related to the type of customer and the customer needs being served by a product or service. *In the standardization of production management, the methods of lean production create visual checkpoints throughout the production process for all aspects of the management function so that communication is immediate and universal.* Heijunka boxes communicate the demand and regulate the flow of production and/or the flow of material withdrawal and use. Kanban cards communicate the demand upstream, ultimately determining raw material ordering and regulating supplier relationships. Visual displays and controls, error-proofing, and quick changeover methods continually decrease work-in-process inventory and defects. *Operators become their own inspectors of both the process and the technical standards.* The ultimate end of lean production is the ability to implement a production system with a high degree of flexibility to respond to changes in customer demand. As regards decision-making, when standards exist, a manager's responsibility becomes easier because everyone knows what to do and how to do it. *Standards support the delegation of responsibility.*

Standards are the foundation of continuous improvement. Without them you cannot focus or measure your improvements. By the time you have implemented a cell layout, quick changeover, and standard work, everyone should have embraced a culture of continuous improvement. Standards and standard work, as we have shown throughout this book, are not static or unchanging. In fact, they are the basis from which improvement changes can be analyzed and tested and then adopted by everyone systematically. They are the content of training efforts—you train people to adhere to both technical and process standards. Standard work, when implemented, creates an even workload for every operator, so that no one works too little or too much, idle time is reduced, and bottlenecks are eliminated. Balanced lines and standard work procedures are the basis for small-lot, level-load production—the ultimate key to customer satisfaction and reduced costs. *In order to set up a pull system using kanban and/or small-lot production using load leveling, standard work is necessary.*

Generally, you will discover that everyone resists standardization until they understand what it really means and how it benefits the company and workers alike. In fact, *100 percent of the time, once standardization is in effect and standard work is in place, creativity, improvement, and job satisfaction increase.* Only after working in an environment where standard work is in place do you discover the advantages to each operator that inevitably result.

Standardization and standard work procedures depend on and derive from all the methods of the lean production system; they bring these methods to their full potential; and they set in motion a continuous improvement cycle for the whole plant that is never ending.

REFLECTIONS

Now that you have completed this chapter, take five minutes to think about these questions and to write down your answers:

- What did you learn from reading this chapter that stands out as particularly useful or interesting?

- Do you have any questions about the topics presented in this chapter? If so, what are they?

- What additional information do you need to fully understand the ideas presented in this chapter?

Chapter 5

Reflections and Conclusions

CHAPTER OVERVIEW

An Implementation Summary for Standard Work

Reflecting on What You've Learned

Opportunities for Further Learning

Conclusions

Additional Resources Related to Standardization and Standard Work

Books and Videos

Newsletters

Training and Consulting

Website

An Implementation Summary for Standard Work

From Standards to Standard Work

Stages of Standards Improvement

1. Diagnose the problem:
   a. Identify and describe the problem. There are two forms of problems—
      i. Variances from established standards
      ii. Variances between actual conditions and improvement goals
   b. Organize the data
   c. Determine the importance of each in terms of advantage derived from solving it

2. Choose the problem you want to address.

3. Set a target for improvement:
   a. How will you know when you have solved the problem?
   b. What measure will indicate that you have solved the problem?

4. Investigate the causes of the problem you are addressing.

5. Draw and describe the current conditions.

6. Brainstorm solutions.

7. Test the solutions until you find the best one:
   a. Run the final solution through the process
   b. Check and adjust until the problem is permanently solved

8. Establish the new standard.

Steps to Achieving Standard Work

1. Create a Parts Production Capacity Worktable.

2. Create a Standard Operations Combination Chart.

3. Create a Work Methods Chart.

4. Create a Standard Operations Chart.

5. Create a visual display of the charts.

6. Create Standard Operations Pointers Charts for future problem solving.

7. Focus ongoing improvement activities on the following areas:
   a. Flow of materials
   b. Multi-skilled layout and operators
   c. Motion in operations
   d. Equipment
   e. Separation of machine operations from manual operations
   f. Defect prevention

Guidelines for Maintaining Standard Operations (Standardization)

1. Establish standard operations universally throughout the factory, which are completely supported by top management.

2. Make sure everyone understands the importance of standard operations—from the president to the newest employee.

3. See that workshop leaders and anyone responsible for training others in standard operations are confident in and committed to the standard operations they teach.

4. Post visual displays to remind everyone of the importance of adhering to the standards.

5. Post graphic and text descriptions of the standard operations so that workers can compare their own work to the standards.

6. Bring in a third party to clear up any misunderstandings.

7. Hold workshop leaders responsible for maintaining standard work.

8. Reject the status quo. Remember that improvement never ends, and continually look for ways to improve the existing standards.

9. Conduct small group improvement activities regularly to gather new ideas and alert one another to problems as they arise.

10. Systematically pursue the establishment of a new, higher level of standard work.

Reflecting on What You've Learned

Key Point

An important part of learning is reflecting on what you've learned. Without this step, learning can't take place effectively. That's why we've asked you to reflect at the end of each chapter. And now that you've reached the end of the book, we'd like to ask you to reflect on what you've learned from the book as a whole.

Take ten minutes to think about the following questions and to write down your answers:

- What did you learn from reading this book that stands out as particularly useful or interesting?

- What ideas, concepts, and techniques have you learned that will be *most* useful to you during implementation of standard work? How will they be useful?

- What ideas, concepts, and techniques have you learned that will be *least* useful during implementation of standard work? Why won't they be useful?

- Do you have any questions about standard work? If so, what are they?

Opportunities for Further Learning

How-to Steps

Here are some ways to learn more about standard work:

- Find other books, videos, or trainings on this subject. Several are listed on the next pages.

- If your company is already implementing standard work, visit other departments or areas to see how they are applying the ideas and approaches you have learned about here.

- Find out how other companies have implemented standard work. You can do this by reading magazines and books about standard work, and by attending conferences and seminars presented by others.

Conclusions

Standardization and standard work are more than a series of techniques. They are a fundamental approach to improving the manufacturing process. We hope this book has given you a taste of how and why this approach can be helpful and effective for you in your work.

Additional Resources Related to Standardization and Standard Work

Books and Videos

Waste Reduction and Lean Manufacturing Methods

Shigerhiro Nakamura, *The New Standardization: Keystone of Continuous Improvement in Manufacturing* (Productivity Press, 1993). This book offers detailed descriptions of the standardization process to be used in every department in a manufacturing company from the shopfloor to top management.

Hiroyuki Hirano, *JIT Implementation Manual: The Complete Guide to Just-in-Time Manufacturing* (Productivity Press, 1990). This two-volume manual is a comprehensive, illustrated guide to every aspect of the lean manufacturing transformation.

Hiroyuki Hirano, *JIT Factory Revolution: A Pictorial Guide to Factory Design of the Future* (Productivity Press, 1988). This book of photographs and diagrams gives an excellent overview of the changes involved in implementing a lean, cellular manufacturing system.

Shigeo Shingo, *A Study of the Toyota Production System: From an Industrial Engineering Viewpoint* (Productivity Press, 1989). This classic book was written by the renowned industrial engineer who helped develop key elements of the Toyota system's success.

Jeffrey Liker, *Becoming Lean: Inside Stories of U.S. Manufacturers* (Productivity Press, 1997). This book shares powerful first-hand accounts of the complete process of implementing cellular manufacturing, just-in-time, and other aspects of lean production.

Japan Management Association (ed.), *Kanban and Just-in-Time at Toyota: Management Begins at the Workplace* (Productivity Press, 1986). This classic overview book describes the underlying concepts and main techniques of the original lean manufacturing system.

Taiichi Ohno, *Toyota Production System: Beyond Large-Scale Production* (Productivity Press, 1988). This is the story of the first lean manufacturing system, told by the Toyota vice president who was responsible for implementing it.

Ken'ichi Sekine, *One-Piece Flow: Cell Design for Transforming the Production Process* (Productivity Press, 1992). This comprehensive book describes how to redesign the factory layout for the most effective deployment of equipment and people; it includes many examples and illustrations.

Iwao Kobayashi, *20 Keys to Workplace Improvement* (Productivity Press, 1995). This book addresses 20 key areas in which a company must improve to maintain a world class manufacturing operation. A five-step improvement for each key is described and illustrated.

The 5S System and Visual Management

Tel-A-Train and the Productivity Press Development Team, *The 5S System: Workplace Organization and Standardization* (Tel-A-Train, 1997). Filmed at leading U.S. companies, this seven-tape training package (co-produced with Productivity Press) teaches shopfloor teams how to implement the 5S System.

Productivity Press Development Team, *5S for Operators: Five Pillars of the Visual Workplace* (Productivity Press, 1996). This Shopfloor Series book outlines five key principles for creating a clean, visually organized workplace that is easy and safe to work in. Contains numerous tools, illustrated examples, and how-to steps, as well as discussion questions and other learning features.

Michel Greif, *The Visual Factory: Building Participation Through Shared Information* (Productivity Press, 1991). This book shows how visual management techniques can provide just-in-time information to support teamwork and employee participation on the factory floor.

Quick Changeover

Productivity Press Development Team, *Quick Changeover for Operators: The SMED System* (Productivity Press, 1996). This Shopfloor Series book describes the stages of changeover improvement with examples and illustrations.

Shigeo Shingo, *A Revolution in Manufacturing: The SMED System* (Productivity Press, 1985). This classic book tells the story of Shingo's SMED System, describes how to implement it, and provides many changeover improvement examples.

Poka-Yoke (Mistake-Proofing) and Zero Quality Control

Productivity Press Development Team, *Mistake-Proofing for Operators: The ZQC System* (Productivity Press, 1997). This Shopfloor Series book describes the basic theory behind mistake-proofing and introduces poka-yoke systems for preventing errors that lead to defects.

Shigeo Shingo, *Zero Quality Control: Source Inspection and the Poka-Yoke System* (Productivity Press, 1986). This classic book tells how Shingo developed his ZQC approach. It includes a detailed introduction to poka-yoke devices and many examples of their application in different situations.

NKS/Factory Magazine (ed.), *Poka-Yoke: Improving Product Quality by Preventing Defects* (Productivity Press, 1988). This illustrated book shares 240 poka-yoke examples implemented at different companies to catch errors and prevent defects.

C. Martin Hinckley, *Make No Mistake! An Outcome-Based Approach to Mistake-Proofing* (Productivity Press, 2001). This book sorts all the best methods for preventing defects into an outcome-based classification system to give you the fastest, easiest means for identifying alternative mistake-proofing concepts.

Total Productive Maintenance

Japan Institute of Plant Maintenance (ed.), *TPM for Every Operator* (Productivity Press, 1996). This Shopfloor Series book introduces basic concepts of TPM, with emphasis on the six big equipment-related losses, autonomous maintenance activities, and safety.

Japan Institute of Plant Maintenance (ed.), *Autonomous Maintenance for Operators* (Productivity Press, 1997). This Shopfloor Series book on key autonomous maintenance activities includes chapters on cleaning/inspection, lubrication, localized containment of contamination, and one-point lessons related to maintenance.

Quality Improvement Methods

Yoji Akao (ed.), *Quality Function Deployment: Integrating Customer Requirements into Product Design* (Productivity Press, 1990). This book shows how to satisfy customer needs and expectations by translating them into design targets and quality assurance points and then deploying them through product design, parts selection, and process design. It includes case studies, detailed charts, and over 100 diagrams.

John R. Hartley, *Concurrent Engineering: Shortening Lead Times, Raising Quality, and Lowering Costs* (Productivity Press, 1998). By simultaneously examining the concerns of design, finance, and marketing from the very first stages of production planning, concurrent engineering makes doing it right the first time the rule instead of the exception. Contains sixteen clear guidelines for achieving concurrent engineering, and abundant case studies.

Takashi Ichida, *Product Design Review: A Method for Error-Free Product Development* (Productivity Press, 1996). This book leads you through the basic steps in design review and highlights the nuances of this important quality assurance methodology to foresee and circumvent virtually all of the problems that can plague the development process. Presents a systematic methodology and case studies.

Kenichi Sekine and Keisuke Arai, *Design Team Revolution: How to Cut Lead Times in Half and Double Your Productivity* (Productivity Press, 1994). Exploring each area of the design process in detail, this book shows how to transform designers from isolated multi-project employees to team-based, production-style workers to bring about the maximum productivity of your design department.

Newsletters

Lean Manufacturing Advisor—News and case studies on how companies are implementing lean manufacturing philosophy and specific techniques such as pull production, kanban, cell design, and so on. For subscription information, call 1-800-394-6868.

Training and Consulting

Productivity Consulting Group offers a full range of consulting and training services on lean manufacturing approaches. For additional information, call 1-800-394-6868.

Website

Visit our web pages at www.productivityinc.com to learn more about Productivity's products and services related to standard work.

About the Productivity Press Development Team

Since 1979, Productivity, Inc. has been publishing and teaching the world's best methods for achieving manufacturing excellence. At the core of this effort is a team of dedicated product developers, including writers, instructional designers, editors, and producers, as well as content experts with years of experience in the field. Hands-on experience and networking keep the team in touch with changes in manufacturing as well as in knowledge sharing and delivery. The team also learns from customers and applies this knowledge to create effective vehicles that serve the learning needs of every level in the organization.

About the Shopfloor Series

Put powerful and proven improvement tools in the hands of your entire workforce!

Progressive shopfloor improvement techniques are imperative for manufacturers who want to stay competitive and to achieve world class excellence. And it's the comprehensive education of all shopfloor workers that ensures full participation and success when implementing new programs. The Shopfloor Series books make practical information accessible to everyone by presenting major concepts and tools in simple, clear language.

Books currently in the Shopfloor Series include:

5S FOR OPERATORS
5 Pillars of the Visual Workplace
The Productivity Press Development Team
ISBN 1-56327-123-0 / 133 pages
Order 5SOP-BK / $25.00

QUICK CHANGEOVER FOR OPERATORS
The SMED System
The Productivity Press Development Team
ISBN 1-56327-125-7 / 93 pages
Order QCOOP-BK / $25.00

MISTAKE-PROOFING FOR OPERATORS
The Productivity Press Development Team
ISBN 1-56327-127-3 / 93 pages
Order ZQCOP-BK / $25.00

JUST-IN-TIME FOR OPERATORS
The Productivity Press Development Team
ISBN 1-56327-134-6 / 96 pages
Order JITOP-BK / $25.00

TPM FOR EVERY OPERATOR
The Japan Institute of Plant Maintenance
ISBN 1-56327-080-3 / 136 pages
Order TPMEO-BK / $25.00

TPM FOR SUPERVISORS
The Productivity Press Development Team
ISBN 1-56327-161-3 / 96 pages
Order TPMSUP-BK / $25.00

TPM TEAM GUIDE
Kunio Shirose
ISBN 1-56327-079-X / 175 pages
Order TGUIDE-BK / $25.00

AUTONOMOUS MAINTENANCE
The Japan Institute of Plant Maintenance
ISBN 1-56327-082-x / 138 pages
Order AUTOMOP-BK / $25.00

FOCUSED EQUIPMENT IMPROVEMENT FOR TPM TEAMS
The Japan Institute of Plant Maintenance
ISBN 1-56327-081-1 / 144 pages
Order FEIOP-BK / $25.00

OEE FOR OPERATORS
The Productivity Press Development Team
ISBN 1-56327-221-0 / 96 pages
Order OEEOP-BK / $25.00

CELLULAR MANUFACTURING
One-Piece Flow for Workteams
The Productivity Press Development Team
ISBN 1-56327-213-X / 96 pages
Order CELL-BK / $25.00

KANBAN FOR THE SHOPFLOOR
The Productivity Press Development Team
ISBN 1-56327-269-5 / 120 pages
Order KANOP-BK / $25.00

KAIZEN FOR THE SHOPFLOOR
The Productivity Press Development Team
ISBN 1-56327-272-5 / 112 pages
Order KAIZOP-BK / $25.00

PULL PRODUCTION FOR THE SHOPFLOOR
The Productivity Press Development Team
ISBN 1-56327-274-1 / 122 pages
Order PULLOP-BK / $25.00

STANDARD WORK FOR THE SHOPFLOOR
The Productivity Press Development Team
ISBN 1-56327-273-3 / 112 pages
Order STANOP-BK / $25.00

Productivity Press, 444 Park Avenue South, Suite 604, New York, NY 10016
Customer Service Department: Telephone **1-800-394-6868** Fax **1-800-394-6286**

THE SHOPFLOOR SERIES LEARNING ASSESSMENT PACKAGE

Software to Confirm the Learning of Your Knowledge Workers

Created by the Productivity Development Team

How do you know your employee education program is getting results? Employers need to be able to quantify the benefit of their investment in workplace education. The *Shopfloor Series books* and *Learning Packages* from Productivity Press offer a simple, cost-effective approach for building basic knowledge about key manufacturing improvement topics. Now you can confirm the learning with the *Shopfloor Series Learning Assessment*.

The *Shopfloor Series Learning Assessment* is a new software package developed specifically to complement five key books in the *Shopfloor Series*. Each module of the Learning Assessment provides knowledge tests based on the contents of one of the *Shopfloor Series books*, which are written for production workers. After an employee answers the questions for a chapter in the book, the software records his or her score. Certificates are included for recognizing the employee's completion of the assessment for individual modules and for all five core modules.

The *Shopfloor Series Learning Assessment* will help your company ensure that employees are learning and are recognized and rewarded for gaining knowledge. It supports professional development for your employees as well as effective implementation of shopfloor improvement programs.

ISBN 1-56327-203-2
Order ASSESS-BK / $1495.00

Here's How the Learning Assessment Package Works:

1. The employee reads one of the Shopfloor Series books, chapter by chapter. Easy to read and understand, the books educate your employees with information they need, and prepare them for the learning assessment test questions.

2. After an administrator has set up the Learning Assessment software on a computer, the employee can then use the computer to answer a set of test questions about the information in the Shopfloor Series book they have read. The software automatically scores the answers and logs the score into a database for easy access by the administrator.

3. If the employee does not pass the assessment for a particular chapter, he or she can review the material in the book and take the assessment again. (For security, the software selects randomly from three different questions on each topic.)

4. Upon passing the assessment modules for all chapters of the Shopfloor Series books, the employee receives a completion certificate (included in the package) and any other reward or recognition determined by your company.

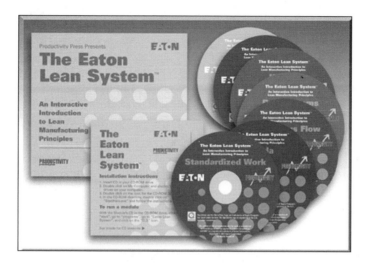

THE EATON LEAN SYSTEM

An Interactive Introduction to Lean Manufacturing Principles

If you're interested in a multi-media learning package, the best one available is *The Eaton Lean System*. Integrating the latest in interactivity with informative and powerful video presentations, this innovative software involves the user at every level. Nowhere else will you find the fundamental concepts of lean so accessible and interesting. Seven topic-focused CDs let you tackle lean subjects in the order you choose. Graphs, clocks, and diagrams showing time wasted or dollars lost powerfully demonstrate the purpose of lean. Video clips show real people working either the lean way or the wasteful way. Easy to install and use, *The Eaton Lean System* offers the user exceptional flexibility. Either interact with the program on your own, or involve a whole group by using an LCD display.

This Software Package Includes:

7 CDs covering these important lean concepts!

- Muda
- Standardized Work
- Continuous Flow
- 5S (including 5S for administrative areas)
- Pull Systems
- Kaizen
- Heijunka

Includes in-plant video footage, interactive exercises, and extensive simulations!

System Requirements — PC Compatible

Microsoft Windows® '98
8MB Free RAM

QuickTime for Windows 32 bit
16 bit display

The Eaton Lean System
The Productivity Development Team
ISBN 1-56327-261-X
Order EATON-BK / $695.00

Books from Productivity, Inc.

Productivity Press publishes books that empower individuals and companies to achieve excellence in quality, productivity, and the creative involvement of all employees. Through steadfast efforts to support the vision and strategy of continuous improvement, Productivity Press delivers today's leading-edge tools and techniques gathered directly from industry leaders around the world.

To request a complete catalog of our publications call us toll free at **800-394-6868** or visit us online at www.productivityinc.com

THE NEW STANDARDIZATION—KEYSTONE OF CONTINUOUS IMPROVEMENT IN MANUFACTURING

Shigehiro Nakamura

In an era of continuous improvement and ISO 9000, quality is not an option but a requirement—and you can't set or meet criteria for quality without standardization. Standardization lets you share information about the best ways to do things so that they will be done that way consistently. This book shows how to make standardization a living system of just-in-time information that delivers exactly the information that's needed, exactly when it is needed, and exactly where it is needed. It's the only way to sustain the results of your improvement efforts in every area of your company.

ISBN 1-56327-251-2 / 284 pages / $40.00 / Stock # STANDP-BK

VALUE STREAM MANAGEMENT—EIGHT STEPS TO PLANNING, MAPPING, AND SUSTAINING LEAN IMPROVEMENTS

Don Tapping, Tom Luyster, and Tom Shuker

Value stream management is a complete system that provides a clear path to lean implementation, ensuring quick deployment and great benefits. *Value Stream Management—Eight Steps to Planning, Mapping, and Sustaining Lean Improvements* shows you how to use mapping as part of a complete system for lean implementation. The central feature of this illustrative and engaging book is the value stream management storyboard, a tool representing an eight-step process for lean implementation. The storyboard brings together people, tools, metrics, and reporting into one visual document.

ISBN 1-56327-245-8 / 169 pages / $45.00 / Stock # VALUE-BK

REORGANIZING THE FACTORY: COMPETING THROUGH CELLULAR MANUFACTURING

Nancy Hyer and Urban Wemmerlöv

Cellular manufacturing principles, applied to either administrative work or production, are fundamental building blocks for lean and quick response organizations. *Reorganizing the Factory* is the definitive reference book in this important area. *Reorganizing the Factory*'s detailed and comprehensive "life cycle" approach will take readers from basic concepts and advantages of cells through the process of justifying, designing, implementing, operating, and improving this new type of work organization in each unique environment.

ISBN 1-56327-228-8 / 784 pages / $90.00 / Stock # REORG-BK

FAST TRACK TO WASTE-FREE MANUFACTURING—STRAIGHT TALK FROM A PLANT MANAGER

John W. Davis

Now available in text and audio book formats!*

Batch, or mass, manufacturing is still the preferred system of production for most U.S.-based industry. But to survive, let alone become globally competitive, companies will have to put aside their old habitual mass manufacturing paradigms and completely change their existing system of production. In *Fast Track to Waste-Free Manufacturing: Straight Talk from a Plant Manager*, John Davis details a new and proven system called Waste-Free Manufacturing (WFM) that rapidly deploys the lean process. He covers nearly every aspect of the lean revolution and provides essential tools and techniques you will need to implement WFM. Drawing from more than 30 years of manufacturing experience, John Davis gives you tools and techniques for eliminating anything that cannot be clearly established as value added.

Text Format: ISBN: 1-56327-212-1 / 425 pages / $45.00 / Stock # WFM-BK

Audio book format:

On 4 audio CDs:
ISBN: 1-56327-279-2 / $37.95 / 296 minutes / Stock # FASTCD-BK
On 4 audio cassettes:
ISBN: 1-56327-278-4 / $37.95 / 296 minutes / Stock # FASTTP-BK

*The audio version is an abridgement of the original text edition.

352852

6032

PROCESS MASTERING—HOW TO ESTABLISH AND DOCUMENT THE BEST KNOWN WAY TO DO A JOB

Ray W. Wilson and Paul Harsin

This book offers a method to create a continuous improvement document—the "Process Master." This new quality tool documents all the facets of a process as they actually occur—steps, inputs, outputs, equipment, controls—utilizing the "untapped" process knowledge of your organization's workforce. It allows you to standardize a procedure, which then can be easily reviewed and improved. The benefits include cost reduction, increased productivity, improved safety, higher morale, and the ability to meet the changing expectations of your customers.

ISBN 0-527-76344-6 / 168 pages / $24.00 / Stock # MASTER-BK

ONE-PIECE FLOW—CELL DESIGN FOR TRANSFORMING THE PRODUCTION PROCESS

Kenichi Sekine

By reconfiguring your traditional assembly lines into production cells based on one-piece flow, you can drastically reduce your lead time, staffing requirements, and number of defects. Sekine examines the basic principles of process flow building, then offers detailed case studies of how various industries designed unique one-piece flow systems to meet their particular needs.

ISBN 0-915299-33-X / 308 pages / $75.00 / Stock # 1PIECE-BK

TOYOTA PRODUCTION SYSTEM—BEYOND LARGE-SCALE PRODUCTION

Taiichi Ohno

Now available in text and audio book formats!

Taiichi Ohno is considered the inventor of the Toyota Production System (known as Just-In-Time manufacturing) and lean manufacturing. In *Toyota Production System*, the creator of just-in-time production for Toyota reveals the origins, daring innovations and ceaseless evolution of the Toyota system into a full management system.

Text Format: ISBN 0-915299-14-3 / 143 pages / $45.00 / Stock #: OTPS-BK

Audio book format:

   On 3 audio CDs:
   ISBN: 1-56327-267-9 / $23.00 / 180 minutes / Stock # OHNOCD-BK
   On 2 audio cassettes:
   ISBN: 1-56327-268-7 / $23.00 / 180 minutes / Stock # OHNOTP-BK

*The audio version is an abridgement of the original text edition.